If I were a Blackbird ...

Recollections of Old Stevenage

For Naomi, Stephen and Dominic

If I were a Blackbird ...

Recollections of Old Stevenage

– David Wallis –

Fern House

First published in 2005 by
Fern House
High Street   Haddenham
ELY Cambridgeshire CB6 3XA

www.fernhouse.com

ISBN 1 902702 11 5

Jacket design and text layout by Charlotte Edwards.
Printed in England by TJ International Ltd, Padstow.

CONTENTS

LIST OF ILLUSTRATIONS

List of illustrations

ACKNOWLEDGEMENTS

I am very greatful to the many people who have given me help, advice and encouragement and contributed material towards the writing of this book. Without them, and without the stimulation provided by the local histories of Reginald Hine, Margaret Ashby and Robert Trow-Smith, as well as the remarkable sociological study by Harold Orlans and the history of Alleyne's Grammar School by Dorothy de Salis and Richard Stephens, it could scarcely have been written.

In particular, I would like to thank Frances Jo MacKeith, Verula Rogers, Frances Bygrave, Clifford Culpin and Howard Culpin for information on the Culpin family; Mary Wallis for research on the Culpin and Wallis family trees; Sally Ackroyd and Claire Hill of Stevenage Museum for their support and helpful suggestions; Vic Folbigg and Dennis Taylor for permission to use material from Lummy's Scrapbook; Clive Abrey of Stevenage Borough FC for permission to use their photographs; Frank Hartles for his photographic expertise; Darren Isted, Comet Newspapers, for permission to use reports and pictures from the *Hertfordshire Express* and *Herts Pictorial;* Margaret Ashby for permission to use material from *The Book of Stevenage* and Richard Stephens for permission to use material from 'An innings well played' and 'Happy are thy men'; Nina Hamburger for her constant support and unflagging interest.

I am also indebted to the following for permission from: Stevenage Museum to reproduce photographs, use them as the basis of drawings, and quote from their publications; Mrs R B H Vellender to cite *Tall Nettles*; Everyman's Library to quote from poems by John Clare; Joan Catteau to quote from *Stevenage Voices;* *The Listener* to quote from EM Forster's talk; *the American Psychological Association* to quote from *Millais Culpin : An*

Acknowledgements

Autobiography, and the Souvenir Press to quote from Daniel Schacter's *The seven sins of memory.*

Taylor & Francis and Harper Collins raised no objections to the use of extracts from Reginald Hine : *Hitchin Worthies* or Harold Orlans : Stevenage. *A Sociological Study of a New Town,* respectively.

We have done our best to trace the Copyright Holders but apologise for any errors or omissions, which will be corrected in subsequent editions.

INTRODUCTION

Nothing much happened to Stevenage! No great battles were fought there. The Anglo-Saxons and the Danes didn't wage war over the town. The Black Death may have overlooked it. Oliver Cromwell never chased Charles the First there and the Fuehrer didn't really bother to bomb it. True, the Romans left six roadside tumuli along the Great North Road, Pepys paid a brief visit and Dickens used to come to Stevenage on his way to meet the Lyttons at Knebworth House. But less momentous things which have shaped its individual local history happened all the time. Some of these events have resonated in my memory to determine the shape and chapters of this book. Perhaps I have dwelt on them at too great a length, but my intention was to carry the reader back to the ethos and milieu of a small country town poised on the lip of change. Set in a district which E M Forster thought 'the loveliest in England ... It is agricultural land and could not be described in terms of beauty spots ... It must always have looked much the same,' the town and its inhabitants were about to encounter the Second World War and, soon after, the transforming plans for the creation of a New Town.

A name, a photograph or a passage in a book has triggered a tranche of recollections to do with the countryside, the Methodist Church in Stevenage, the disputes over the New Town Plan, my mother's family the Culpins, the Town Football club or the local grammar school. Perhaps these are the more deeply embedded in my brain because the events happened during my childhood and early youth. This book is a personal account of the Stevenage I remember, an attempt to look back in tranquillity at various aspects of the town and its people which were most significant for the Wallis family. 50 years later they depict a Stevenage lost beneath the flyovers and the underpasses.

In 1945 I was eleven years old and Stevenage was a small town of about 6,000 people so nestled in the countryside that meadows bordered parts of Fairview Road. We lived in No.98 which abutted onto allotments and an acre or two of waste land, a natural playground for children. This rural setting provides the basis of the pastoral of Chapters 1 and 2. The outbreak of war forced a more productive agriculture on the fields and farmers of Stevenage. Land was needed for arable crops. Heavy horses came out of retirement to pull carts and farm machinery. The hamlets in the countryside around the town formed 'greens': Fishers Green, Symonds Green, Norton Green, and so on. Some of the most attractive of the surviving cottages and farms were to be found on these greens and are shown in the drawings.

For the Wallis family the Methodist Church played a central part in family life. Grandpa Wallis was a lay preacher and sang in the choir. So did my dad, who was also a local officer, a circuit steward of the church. It is easy to forget the extent to which church events – choir practice, Sunday school, youth groups, guild meetings – structured the social life of the week and of the year. The most colourful annual event was the Harvest Festival. Then the whole church was bedecked with fruits, vegetables and corn in a profusion of autumn produce.

The Second World War brought its own excitements with dramas that were usually low key. Soldiers and convoys came and went, an anti-aircraft battery was set up in the allotments and Italian Prisoners-of-War came to work in the fields. My mother kept a diary during the war; Dad joined the Home Guard and found himself in the Signals Section. Fairview Road and all its houses survived the war only to be demolished on paper in the Plans for the New Town. Protest meetings and legal action, rotten fruit hurled at the Minister of Housing, prevarication and delay, led to a very unsettled period for Stevenage. The arguments which raged backwards and forwards, the attitudes of the parties for and against the New Town Scheme, provide a microcosm of progress and reaction to change in a changing Britain. The issues were not black and white; the New Town was no utopia, nor was Old Stevenage a rural eden. Inevitably, the upshot was a compromise. Events in Stevenage must be viewed against a background of a desperate need for new housing and the requirement to re-house people displaced by wartime bombing. In the end, Fairview Road and its houses, but not alas its meadows, survived to the present day.

My mother's family has its own rich history. I am still tracing it back through the Seventeenth Century. The Culpins have thrown up interesting odd-balls and experts, medics, scientists and architects, romantics and dissenters. I felt they deserved two chapters to themselves, partly because of the contributions of my Great Uncle Millais Culpin to Industrial Psychology. During my childhood, my Grandmother Culpin's house at 5 Basils Road seemed the perfect retreat, the centre around which my wider family revolved. It was here we came for Christmas parties, here in Spring that the cherry tree outside the kitchen window produced sweet red fruit, and here behind the apple orchard that the revolving summer-house sat with its stifling smells of honey and beeswax.

Introduction

The Wallis family came from Dorset via London; my great-grandfather was a sergeant in the Dorset police. Photographs but not much narrative detail survive about the family in Stevenage, apart from those to do with Auntie Nellie's family. Auntie Nelly and Uncle Albert lived just up from the High Street; some of my clearest memories are of Saturday morning shopping trips along Stevenage High Street and visits to Stevenage Fair.

Punctuating the prolonged crisis over the development of the New Town were episodes of football fever. The Town Football Club propelled itself with fervour and self-belief into famous games in the F A Amateur Cup against Wimbledon, Corinthian Casuals and Pegasus. One Stevenage hero was Lummy Taylor, dashing down the right wing or playing at centre forward, who kept a scrapbook from these years. This provided a rich source of pictures and press cuttings. The course of these games, even their occurrence, is now scarcely remembered. The sense of occasion and the atmosphere have survived in the descriptions in local newspapers. The words of their reporters provide the period flavour to carry the reader back to those local derbies. For me, the most evocative element is the Stevenage theme song, played over the loud-speaker system at the start of each game which has given this book its title: 'If I were a Blackbird, I'd whistle and sing …'

In the final chapter, I adumbrate the impact of the local Grammar School on my life. It is intended as a tribute both to Alleyne's Grammar School and its dedicated post-war staff who opened all sorts of new horizons for me. Its history illustrates the struggles of a small scholastic institution, founded before Elizabeth I ascended the throne, to survive the vicissitudes of changing local circumstances and government policies.

1

SYMONDS GREEN

MEADOWS

From Fairview Road you could clamber over a stile into Madgin's fields. Before the war these were meadows which were later ploughed up to produce cereals as part of the war effort. Black and white Friesians slumbered in those fields. Sometimes they wandered along the narrow twisting paths between the hawthorn bushes bordering the meadows to the north. Once, when I was a young boy, our golden retriever startled a skylark off her nest in the lush grass, rich with buttercups and oxeye daisies (marguerites). Like a vision a perfect nest with its clutch of olive-brown speckled eggs was laid bare before me.

> Her eggs were four of dusky hue,
> Blotched brown as is the very ground,
> With tinges of a purply hue
> The larger ends encircling round.
>
> – John Clare [1]

These fields in summer were full-choired with birds.

> Hark how the cheerful birds do chant their lays
> And carol of love's praise.
> The merry lark her matins sings aloft,
> The thrush replies, the mavis descant plays.
>
> – Edmund Spenser [2]

The hedges replete with linnets and finches were bright with may blossom in Spring. These were all dug out and the stumps and brushwood burnt early in the war. Prisoners of war – mainly Italian I think – were drafted in to do the navvying work. Cheery, happy to have left the conflict, friendly even, could these be the men who had been harassing the British Army?

The war seemed vastly remote, as if fought in a far off country in another time, even though our school classroom had maps on the walls charting the progress through North Africa of Montgomery and Co. The scars left by the vanished hedgerows and the piles of woodash which bore testament to the funeral pyres soon faded. Purple willow herb, primroses and violets filled them, grass and shrubs returned to provide cover for numerous buntings, yellowhammers and other birds. The bushes soon grew big enough to provide nesting sites for blackbirds, thrushes and finches. With the clearing of the land, a rotation of crops started. To the farmers this was a return to drudgery, because petrol and diesel were scarcely obtainable. The fields had to be ploughed, harrowed and drilled by horse-drawn machines, dug from dusty, nettle-grown backyards.

> Tall nettles cover up, as they have done
> These many springs, the rusty harrow, the plough
> Long worn out, and the roller made of stone
> Only the elm butt tops the nettles now.
>
> This corner of the farmyard I like most:
> As well as any bloom upon a flower
> I like the dust on the nettles, never lost
> Except to prove the sweetness of a shower.
>   – Edward Thomas *Tall Nettles* [3]

The Madgins had just such a museum yard behind the White Lion pub, complete with 'thirties' decrepit open-platform lorries which from time to time were cajoled back into service. But the cutting and binding into sheaves of the corn – mainly wheat, sometimes barley or oats – was done by the horse-drawn machines. For those that watched, a happy return to prewar ways.

When the corn had been bound into sheaves, the sheaves had to be stacked into stooks to dry and ripen further. Then came threshing, mostly done in a corner of the same fields – a festive occasion. The antiquated threshing machine, temperamental and unpowered, needed to be driven by belts attached to a donkey engine or a steam farm engine, a marvellous, smoking, whizzing and fizzing machine, too heavy to cross the field except when the ground was firm and dry. The pulleys could power two or more belt drives, one feeding an elevator which took the sheaves to the heart of the threshing machine where they were flailed to separate the grain. The straw emerged as a kind of waste product, but the grain was fed down chutes to a succession of hessian sacks or sometimes into the back of a truck. The whole scene was noisy and dusty, but full of purposeful activity. It was machinery that had sense – each component with a clearly discernible function obvious from its design. A boy could spend a whole day watching each stage, larking in the noise and the dust. There was a palpable air of successfully bringing the harvest home. The golden Naples Yellow straw was carefully built into stacks, a feature of these fields, comfy nests for country lovers.

These scenes were fleeting moments in the long, tedious war years. Later some diesel oil became available. Bob Madgin, the eldest son of the farming family, returned from the war. He was able to dash about in a bright red, brand new Massey–Harris tractor. The days of the horse-drawn reaper–binder were clearly over. The glamour conferred by the bright red tractor allowed the courtship of the smart befringed daughter of our next door neighbour!

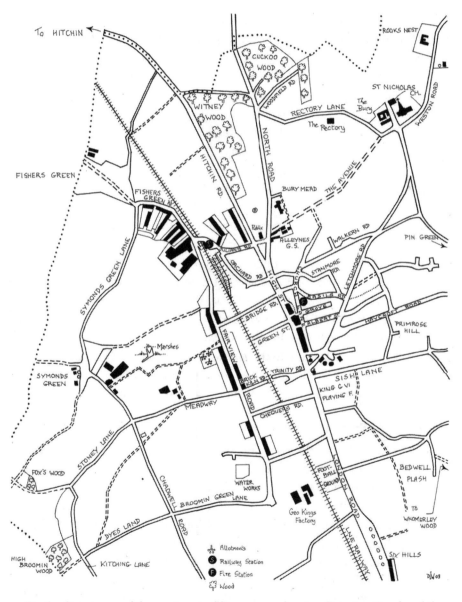

Fig 1 – Street map of the west part of Stevenage, showing Fairview Road and the Town Centre. The map has been re-drawn from a map in the Official Guide to Stevenage for 1946. The dotted line shows the boundary of the Urban District.

FOXES WOOD

Cross now the stile which takes you on the path towards the Oakmead Nurseries. Through a large open field visited by lapwings, you reach Meadway Lane, and a little way along a crossroads with Chadwell Road at which mongrel collies from Gates' farm sometimes prowled to attack the unwary stroller. Go up the unmade track, Stoney Lane – a hot, rutted cartway ascending the hill towards Foxes Wood which sits on the horizon. This was really a copse rather than a wood. The copse, roughly triangular in shape and lying just to the north of High Broomin Wood, is unnamed on Ordinance Survey maps. It may have been called Foxes Wood in local parlance, not because of the Fox twins but because it was one of the covers and spinneys set aside for foxes by hunting landlords at the period of the enclosures[4]. In Spring, the tree roots were awash with azure blue. Foxes Wood was one of the many bluebell woods around Stevenage. Whomerly (Umbley) Wood and Sishes Wood were two others towards which we would pilgrimage. Mary Spicer[5] describes the woods as 'carpeted with anemones and primroses. Later ... the verdant green of dog's mercury contrasting with .... the bluebells, just as the cherry trees came into blossom overhead.'

From Foxes Wood, a rough path led north-east towards Shepherds Lane and then on to Symonds Green. This was the hamlet where the Fox twins were born. Albert Ebenezer and Ebenezer Albert Fox were celebrated poachers whose colourful history, perhaps somewhat ornamented, is recorded in *Hitchin Worthies* by the Hitchin historian and antiquarian, Reginald Hine, published in 1932[6]. Ebenezer died in 1926 and Albert in 1937. Reginald Hine was one of only two people present at Albert's funeral, according to the *Hertfordshire Express*. Fate deemed that the twins were born just as partridge shooting began in 1857. The following is based on Hine's account.

THE FOX TWINS

Henry Fox, father of the twins by a third marriage, had fifteen acres of land and a cottage which he leased at Symonds Green. He was a stalwart of the Albert Street Baptist Church and a local or lay preacher. The twins were called Albert after the Chapel and Ebenezer, the name often adopted by Baptists and Methodists for their meeting houses. Both twins attended Sunday School at Albert Street, but Sunday Schools never did reliably breed angels. By the age of ten the twins, Hine says, 'were closely associated with every tree, every hedge, every copse in Stevenage … and no bird's egg was safe within a dozen miles.' Albert Ebenezer and Ebenezer Albert were identical twins impossible to tell apart. Their mother tried different colour ribbons, their father different identifying chairs. 'But ... the ribbon and chair were frequently exchanged; and the father, who was a conscientious man, hardly liked to thrash one child for fear of thrashing the other!'

The law eventually caught up with the twins, 'but always in Court they maintained their youthful air of injured innocence. The summons was based on fabricated evidence – they were not there- the keeper was dreaming – the magistrates were preservers of game and grossly prejudiced – A fine! No, they would pay no bloody fine – they would go to prison, if only as a protest against statutes made for the protection of Esquires.'

The twins had various, often audaciously incredible, lines of defence. One was 'defence by the book' in which the Fox in question would maintain that he was in the said wood at night because he wished to

Fig 2 – The Fox Twins, notorious Stevenage poachers in around 1920 (courtesy Stevenage Museum).

meditate upon the Baptist Hymn Book. 'And that's the truth, the Bible truth and nothing but the truth'. Despite laughter from the Bench, Fox would then fish from his pocket, accompanied by a certain number of feathers, his father's copy of the Baptist Hymn Book. Another line of defence was 'by the bag'. A bag of mushrooms would be thumped down conclusively on the clerk's table as evidence of their legitimate search in the woods for mushrooms. Various tenant farmers were apparently in league with the Foxes and provided them with letters giving written permission to search and take mushrooms in their meadows and woods.

Hine[6] writes of an entry in the records of Hitchin Petty Sessions: 'Sam Hoare, gamekeeper to Sir Charles Nall-Cain, said he found pheasant wires in a break in the hedge at Langley ... and in the wires two pheasants. The next day he resumed watch ... and defendant, Ebenezer Albert Fox, came and went straight to the pheasants. Witness, who was only ten yards away, asked him why he was searching for game. Fox said he was after mushrooms. Witness replied; "What, mushrooms with feathers on ?" Fox, on oath, said that he was twenty yards off the pheasants. He had permission to go into the meadow next to the wood, and he went over the fence separating the wood and the meadow to get some mushrooms, and then the keeper spoke to him. He had some mushrooms in a handkerchief in his hand. He did not see the pheasants until the keeper pointed them out'. The Bench, however, fined him £2 or one month.

A better defence was that of mistaken identity. Poaching separately allowed each to give the name of the other twin when apprehended. In court the defendant would claim that it was his brother, not himself, who should be in the dock. Hine maintains that the Fox twin, whichever it was, would cross-examine the keeper or the constable: 'Have a good look at me, keeper. And now have another look at my brother who is in the Court ... Remember, keeper, you are upon your oath. Don't go and commit perjury please, like you did last time. Now will you swear it was me and not that brother of mine?' The witness would hesitate and was lost, the case would be judged unproven and the twins would leave court grinning contentedly. In broad daylight Sergeant Reynolds of the Stevenage Constabulary would know one from the other, but at night it was nearly impossible to tell them apart. Convicting the twins was so difficult that some landowners bribed the brothers to stay off their land. One lady of the manor offered Albert Ebenezer a pound a week and a brace of pheasants throughout the shooting season to oblige! According to Hine, he took the money and sent his brother instead.

After one longer jail stretch Ebenezer Albert emerged from prison promising a reformed life. He attended the Albert Street Baptist Chapel for a time and helped build the new Stevenage Police Court in Stanmore

Road. But the reformation recorded by Hine was short-lived. 'Though he could lay a brick well enough, he could lay a bird still better'. Times were becoming more difficult for poachers. Fifty flint-stocks, muzzle-loaders and breech-loaders were confiscated from the twins. These were not easy to replace. Ebenezer Albert gradually made fewer forages into the woods. His brother claimed: 'It was all due to the keepers who knocked him about the head. It was their doing that he became deaf and couldn't any longer hear his birds drop.' He ended in Hitchin Infirmary, clothed in Hospital Blue, confined by four walls and hating having to sleep while it was dark. From time to time, Albert would arrive with the latest news and a basket of eggs. But near death Ebenezer wished to get back home. An old poacher had little difficulty in leaving the Infirmary undetected and evading the Hitchin police. At the little village of St Ippolyts on the way to Symonds Green he collapsed from heart failure. He must have crawled into a copse called The Willows where his body was found on 30 September, 1926, by Superintendent Prior. He is buried in Stevenage in the churchyard of St Nicholas.

Hine, well-acquainted with the twins, describes Albert Ebenezer still hale and hearty five years later, though rumoured to be dead – sitting in the snug of The Crooked Billet at Symonds Green, eyes blinking at the unaccustomed daylight. His puckered rotund face had altered little over the years, weathered to a ruddy-brown, the bullet head was 'as bald and brown as a partridge's egg and sitting squash down without a neck upon his bullet-shaped body; the same old ears splayed out as if made to catch sounds inaudible to civilized and house-abiding men; the same old poacher's coat, all composed of pockets in whose secret recesses a whole covey of partidges could be stowed away.' Hine had frequently encountered Albert Fox in court. He asked him if he was drawing the old-age pension. 'Yes, but what's the use of that, it doesn't keep me in cartridges – they cost tuppence apiece.' He pulled a couple from his pocket. 'I see you use No. 4' said Hine. 'That's right. If you're shooting keepers you need No. 3, but I don't go in for big game now.'

STEVENAGE GREENS

Symonds Green was one of the many Greens around, and especially to the west of, Stevenage: Todds Green, Fishers Green, Broomin Green, Norton Green, Redcoats Green, Rush Green, Pin Green. These were the old clearings and homesteads of the earliest settlements in the pervading woodlands. They existed at a date near to that at which Stevenage itself came into being[7]. Symonds Green had the old manorial name of Woolenwick and was still called Woolwick at the time the Fox twins were born. In the Domesday Book, Woolenwick is said to consist of two estates only slightly more than 100 acres of plough land and a population of smallholders. The hamlet had a substantial amount of timber alongside the arable land and some meadowland where hay could be cut for winter feeding of stock. In 1086, the landlord was the magnate Peter de Valognes, High Sheriff of Hertfordshire and Essex[8]. The green or waste land of the manor was a piece of common land on which the tenants of the manor could pasture their sheep or cattle at certain times of the year[9]. Symonds Green at an early date was absorbed into the manor of Wymondley. In 1581 Edward Symonde obtained some land in Ladyfield, a large open field south of the Green. During the fifteenth century the Green was sometimes called Hickmans Green, Rumbolds Green, sometimes Wolnewyke Grene. Whether the Symond family manor house was near the Green is uncertain. On the Tithe Map of 1834, nine houses appear on the West side of the Green, five being homesteads and four cottages[9]. Twin ponds lay in front of two of the farmhouses which in 1834 were both occupied by members of the Moules Family. The larger of the two farmhouses was a substantial building with an imposing carved oak staircase and may have been the Symond's manor house in earlier times. The old pub, The Crooked Billet, where Hine met Albert Ebenezer Fox, was rebuilt between the wars. It sat beside the road adjacent to two large connected ponds with their contingent of ducks, geese and moorhens.

To an extent the New Town Master Plan for Stevenage of 1949 reflected the presence of these ancient greens: 'The neighbourhood will itself be subdivided into smaller units likely to encourage social relations between families by grouping round commons and greens, in enclosed streets or culs-de-sac, so that people have the chance to meet and come to know each other ... spaces behind the private gardens which will be used communally, where children may play in safety, away from traffic, and yet beside their homes, and where people may sit and meet. These commons, being linked, will form a pleasant means for pedestrians to move about the district[10]. The origin was most probably the 'Reilly' Green or garden common favoured by many planners and a key part of the plans proposed by Sir Charles Reilly for Birkenhead City Council in 1944 'houses round greens, as in pre-Industrial Revolution England'.

THE CROOKED BILLET

There has been a public house at Symonds Green for 150 years and possibly for longer. The Tithe apportionment of 1837 mentions a cottage and garden owned by George Moules and occupied by Elizabeth Moules. In the 1841 Census the cottage is described as a beer shop kept by Elizabeth Moules, who is referred to in the 1851 Census as Beer Shop

Fig 3 – The Crooked Billet Pub, Symonds Green, in 1965 (drawing from a photograph by the author's mother).

Fig 4 – The Crooked Billet in 2003 (photograph by the author).

Keeper[9]. It was the same family who later moved to Stebbing Farm at Fishers Green.

Broomin Green, further to the south, still survives as seven houses in the midst of a factory area. The old manorial name was Brome or Cannix. Protestant Dissenters were allowed to gather here for worship after the 1689 Toleration Act. A Notice of 1737–8 states: 'These are to certify that a congregation of Protestant Dissenters do intend to meet for religious worship at the house of Thomas Impey and Dennis Crown, at Broomin Green in the Parish of Stevenage. Jan 10th. 1737–8.' [8]

Fig 5 – Stebbing Farm at Fishers Green in 1959. Drawing based on a watercolour by the author.

At Fishers Green, flints and Old Stone Age implements were discovered in 1882, evidence of the period when a natural forest of oak, ash and thorn was gradually converted to fertile land. Still heavily wooded, the woods gave place to these farm settlers' clearings and homes, often with names that remain in use to this day. When we boys played cricket on the Green, Stebbing Farm, a few cottages and the Fisherman Public House were the only buildings around the Green. On the approach along Fishers Green Road, there were the somewhat dismal dwellings of the housing development established in the 1890s to produce Jubilee, Huntingdon, Bournemouth and Southsea Roads.

The oldest undisputed site of human habitation in Stevenage is in Whomerly Wood. The remains of a moated farmstead are to be found in a wood very rich in primroses which we would bring back in their sagging bunches to Fairview Road. Whomerley, Homeley, Umbley or Omley, as it appears on the first Ordnance Survey map of 1834, lay at the boundary between Stevenage and Shephall. The name Whomerley derives from the two early English words of 'ham' and 'leah', for house in the clearing.

Fig 6 – Cottage at Fishers Green in 1959. Drawing based on a watercolour by the author.

Fig 7 – Cottage to the west of Stevenage near Lower Titmore Green in around 1958. Drawing based on a watercolour by the author.

The farmstead was almost certainly the house of Ralphe de Homle, who features in the Lay Subsidy Rolls of 1293. The earthworks are the defences of a mediaeval or older home. Trow-Smith[7] describes the site as 'a nearly square entrenchment about eighty yards across, still having on the west and south side a five-foot deep ditch which fills with water in wet weather.' Two small ponds may once have provided water for a mediaeval farmer's stock. A line of flints lies in the neck joining two enclosures, which is all that remains of the buildings or farm path. Excavations have produced mediaeval and Roman pottery.

THE BURY AND THE CHURCH

Signs of Stevenage's Anglo-Saxon heritage survive in the name The Bury (from the Saxon word *burh*, meaning 'a fortified place') and in the 1834 map of Stevenage[8] in which the individual strips grouped in blocks or furlongs of the old open field system can clearly be seen.

Trow-Smith's book *The History of Stevenage*[7] grew from the preliminary notes which Reginald Hine began to make for his own projected history of Stevenage. These drew partly upon original sources and partly upon the writings of E V Methold[11]. Methold built the very distinctive Tower House in Church Lane, often called Back Lane, which runs parallel to the High Street towards the Holy Trinity Church at its south end and heads towards the Avenue and St Nicholas Parish Church at the north end. The small group of houses in which the house stands is shown in the drawing based on a photograph of around 1970.

In the Eighth Century, Stevenage came temporarily under Danish control, while in 1060 Edward the Confessor gave a large plot of land in the region of St Nicholas' church to the monastery of St Peter at Westminster, and 'a small establishment of monks was kept there, who saw to the production and dispatch of vegetables to the parent institutions'. The monastery retained possession until the Dissolution, when the land came to the Crown which soon transferred it to the Bishops of London; in 1868 the Ecclesiastical Commissioners, present Lords of the Manor, received possession[10]. The church stands on high ground half a mile north-east of the town, and somehow or other got away from Stevenage or, according to a legend quoted by E M Forster in Howards End, 'attracted so many worshippers, when the church stood in the village, that the devil, in a pet, snatched it from its foundations, and poised it on an inconvenient knoll'.

Fig 8 – E V Methold's Tower House in Church Lane in around 1970. The house was built in 1895. Drawing by the author from a photograph in Stevenage in Old Photographs[12] *(courtesy of Stevenage Museum).*

Symonds Green

2

BIRDS AND THEIR NESTS

The cornflower is blooming,
The cowslip is coming,
And many new buds on the silken grass lie :
On the earth's shelt'ring breast
Thou has left the brown nest,
And art towering above it, a speck in the sky.

– John Clare [13]

BIRDS' EGGS

In 1949 in my green time, birds' nesting was a passion. With a friend from Symonds Green we would scour the banks, fields and hedgerows for the nests of birds. In years gone by we had collected birds' eggs, piercing each end with a needle and gently blowing out the white and yolk. Taking eggs was frowned upon by naturalists. Collecting eggs was reluctantly abandoned by our newly enlightened selves. That Spring of 1949 I charted the birds' nests found in and around a few of the fields bordering Meadway Lane. I made quick sketches of these nests which could be elaborated upon at home. The pleasure of discovering a nest, re-visiting it to find out how many eggs had been laid, to note the successful hatching and departure of the brood deserves a sweeter pen than mine. John Clare wrote a series of poems[14] about the nests of birds in language fresh and crisp, conveying his utterly personal delight. For him, both Nature and childhood were the proper subjects of poetry. In the Nightingale's Nest he speaks of :

The very spot,
Just where that old man's beard all wildly trails
Rude arbours o'er the road and stops the way –
And where that child its bluebell flowers hath got,
Laughing and creeping through the mossy rails –
These have I haunted like a very boy,
Creeping on hands and knees through matted thorn
To find her nest and see her feed her young.

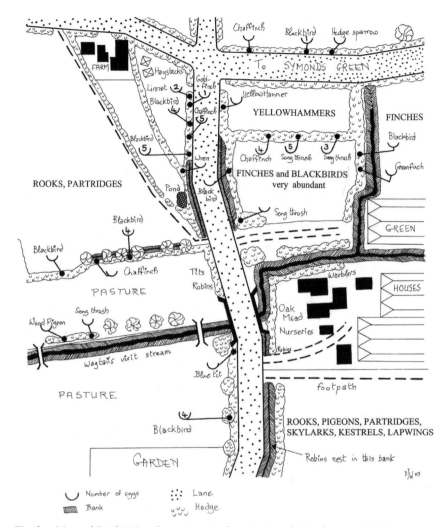

Fig 9 – Map of Birds' Nest locations in the vicinity of Meadway in 1949.

MEADOW PONDS

Most fields had their own secluded pond, screened by trees and bushes, each providing a watering spot for cattle. The clear water was the home of newts and tadpoles, watercrowfoot and water plantain grew there and each pond has its family of moorhens. At one side of the pond, cattle would have churned up the ground where they gained access to the water. Flowering rush and Lady's-smock grew at these margins. Either supported by an overhanging branch, tucked neatly into the bank or on some miniature island or anchored into the reeds, a moorhen's nest could be found. Constructed of twigs and rushes as an open saucer, the boldy spotted eggs held within would be clearly visible. Moorhen chicks are able to take to the water and relative safety as soon as they are hatched, as John Clare puts it:

If I were a Blackbird ...

And still they hatch their eggs and sweetly dream
On their shelfed nest hung just to touch the stream;
And soon their sooty brood from fear elope
Where bulrush forests give them sweeter hope[14].

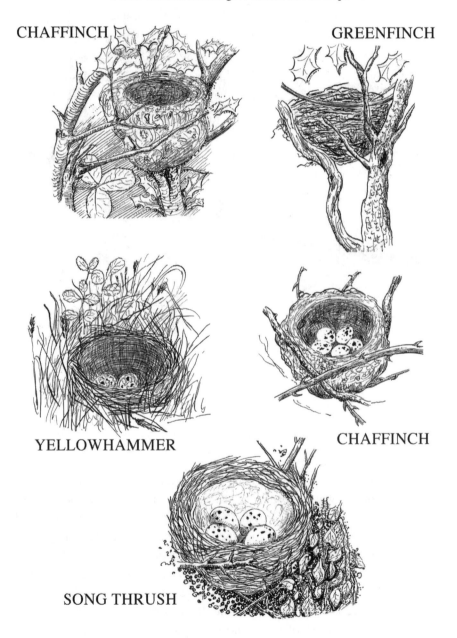

CHAFFINCH

GREENFINCH

YELLOWHAMMER

CHAFFINCH

SONG THRUSH

Fig 10 – Birds' nests drawn in 1949.

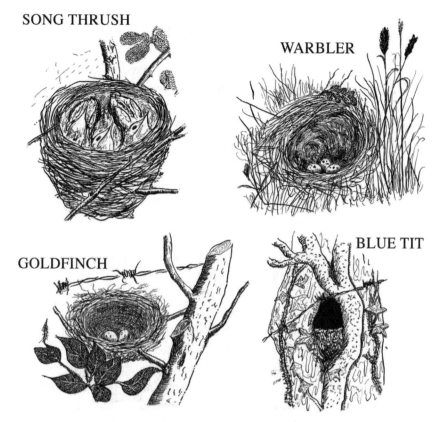

SONG THRUSH

WARBLER

GOLDFINCH

BLUE TIT

Fig 11 – Birds' nests drawn in 1949.

MEADWAY LANE

A thin stream passed through these fields and under Meadway Lane. The hedge bottoms facing this brook provided good protection for nesting birds. The stream supplied water to two commercial nurseries. Oakmead Nurseries abutted onto Meadway Lane and grew mainly tomatoes and cucumbers in hot houses. The source of the stream was a spring near Symonds Green. Symonds Green Nurseries made first use of the brook water, which ran through water meadows known to us as 'the marshes'. These had T-shaped areas that seemed once to have been water cress beds, flooded in winter when their sometimes frozen surface provided an excellent ice-slide, they dried out in summer to become a pot-holed clay morass created by thirsty cattle. Watercress still grew in the stream bed. In a few places, up a highish bank above the stream, were odd remnants of rail, what was left of a small-gauge railway that once must have carried watercress to the Nursery. These archeological remains of the little railway, which left one to imagine what form of locomotive, if any, chuntered along the stream, were more appealing than the intact railway itself might have been.

Yellowhammers were particularly fond of the thick grass, meadow flowers and saplings which grew along the ditches, ditches which were dug out after the hedges in Madgin's fields had been removed. This bird with its yellowish head and body and brown-streaked wings and tail can be easily recognised by its song, which we were taught to identify by the burden: 'A little-bit-of-bread-and-no-cheese'. Her eggs, too, with the inky scrawl marks on their surface are distinctive. John Clare[14] speaks of the yellow-hammer's nest:

> 'Tis rudely planned
> Of bleached stubbles, and the withered fare
> That last year's harvest left upon the land –
> Lined thinly with the horse's sable hair.
> Five eggs, pen-scribbled o'er with ink their shells,
> Resembling writing-scrawls, which fancy reads
> As nature's poesy, and pastoral spells.

THE ALLOTMENTS

Behind 98 Fairview Road lay 'The Allotments'. Reached through the back gardens or by a path further along Fairview Road was an area of grassland and scrub. During the war this was, in part, converted into allotments. The already-enthusiastic gardeners that worked the long back gardens of Fairview Road devoted much time to forcing the rich but weed-riven soil to yield crops of runner beans, broad beans, carrots, cabbages, sprouts and potatoes. The allotment area provided the Fairview Road kids with a playground, the trees and shrubs gave cover for tracking and hide-and-seek games. Here were sites for fabulous child-constructed shelters and defensive earthworks, shelters made of intertwined brushwood and thatched with grass. The bushes were a mixture of hawthorn, blackthorn, dogwood and willow with, fortunately, few brambles. White bryony and convolvulus rambled in places up twiggy escarpments. The tall tussocky clumps of grass, head-high ragwort, mallows, ox-eye daisies, knapweed and deadnettles made this an engaging summer camp. Dandelions grew everywhere, also known as Old man's clock, Jack-piss-the-bed or Wet-the-bed. You could tell the time from dandelion clocks by the number of blows required to remove all the down-covered seeds from the flower head. If you caught one on the wing, you could make a wish. The dandelion's names arose from the diuretic properties of the plant. Because of the high potassium levels of plant tissue, the dandelion serves as a kind of potassium-sparing stimulant of urine production, 'flushing out the kidneys'.

The Allotments were a great place for bird's nests. Chaffinches were always busy there. As Clare[14] has it:

> 'Tis spring, warm glows the south,
> Chaffinch carries moss in his mouth
> To filbert hedges all day long.

Chaffinches, greenfinches, robins, blackbirds, thrushes and wood-pigeons all nested there. A song-thrush's nest could be distinguished from a blackbird's because it was lined with clay and not with moss and grasses. Confirmation came when the blue, black-spotted eggs were laid.

> How true she warped the moss to form the nest,
> And modelled it within with wood and clay;
> And by and by, like heath-bells gilt with dew,
> There lay her shining eggs, as bright as flowers,
> Ink-spotted over shells of greeny blue.
>
> – John Clare[14]

It was at the edge of the allotments, in the corner of an adjoining field, that an anti-aircraft gun was positioned for a period during the war. For the Fairview Road kids this was a source of entertainment and delight, a real life gun with friendly real live gunners. Whether it fired at enemy aircraft I do not know for Stevenage was not bombed during the war, so that the scope for gunnery action must have been limited. A nature diary I kept for 1951 records on 16 May finding a wren's nest built in an old ammunition tin and hanging in a low bush.

HAWTHORN BANKS OFF BRIDGE ROAD

Bridge Road spanned a cutting for the main line to King's Cross. The earth from this must have been deposited in the adjacent field between the railway and the back gardens of houses in Fairview Road to form a sort of plateau about ten feet high, whose banks were covered with hawthorn bushes and whose flat top provided a well drained meadow. The hawthorn is the oldest of the hedgerow trees, the name coming from the Old English word *haga*, meaning 'a hedge' or 'an enclosure'. Hawthorn, whitethorn or quickset was used from Saxon times onward to make impenetrable fences of hedge-thorn[4]. Hawthorn bushes and dog-roses were at their peak in May, glimmering with white may-blossom, providing nesting sites for blackbirds, thrushes and finches, and flooding the summer air with their bitter-sweet smell.

3

STEVENAGE METHODISTS

THE BAND

Thomas Hardy in *Under the Greenwood Tree* recalls the band that performed in the gallery of the village church before the organ arrived to displace it. Unlikely I thought for non-conformist chapels to have a band, even though Stevenage Methodist Church had a disused gallery. But my great-grandfather, Ben Ephraim Lamartine Culpin, describes the band that played in 1856 in the gallery in the previous chapel in the High Street, later converted to a showroom for the Electricity Company. This Chapel, which served as the place of worship until 1876, was built through the generosity of Madame, or variously Mrs or Miss, Harvey of Hinxworth, who:

> At her own expense built chapels at Hinxworth, Baldock and
> Stevenage, and at her death left three thousand pounds to assist
> the spread of Methodism in the dark parts of Hertfordshire.

John Wesley's Journal mentions preaching in Stevenage in 1790 when he was 87, probably in the house of a Mrs Parker. Revd Thomas Vasey, Superintendent of the widespread Bedford Circuit, registered the first Methodist Chapel in Stevenage in 1782. His picture appears in the *Arminian Magazine* (now the *Methodist Magazine*) of that year. The chapel was built by Thomas Allom, gunsmith and clockmaker, the Lay Reader and founder of Methodism in Stevenage. In 1783 he launched an immediate missionary 'attack' on Aston with great initial success. Then smallpox hit the Stevenage Society hard and by 1790 it needed a special visit by John Wesley and financial help from Madame Harvey to restore the cause. The first site for the chapel was adjacent to Thomas Allom's house, possibly near 118 High Street.

According to my great-grandfather, the chief singers sat with the band which included John Moss on bass viol and James Culpin (an uncle of BEL Culpin), who played the flute, and was known throughout the District as 'the Apostle of Solfa'. The band sometimes included an ophicleide – a wind instrument developed from the ancient serpent, a clarinet and a violin. About 1858 Uncle James started a singing class, and when the band was discontinued shortly afterwards, this class became the nucleus for a choir. Singing was started with a tuning fork. Why a gallery, reached by staircases in the west end was included in the design of the new church of 1876 is not clear. It was not used by the choir nor was a new band formed as far as I know. The three arched windows allowing light to the staircase on the south side can be seen in the drawing of the church with the main window which was the principal feature of the west end.

Fig 12 – Stevenage Methodist Church in about 1905. Drawing from a photograph in Stevenage in Old Photographs[12] *– The railings were removed during the Second World War to contribute scrap iron to the war effort. On the left of the picture can be seen an end gable and chimney of the Coach and Horses Public House. The present shabby building, whose portico and west end entrance has been sealed off, is a sad relic of the building as it was at the beginning of the century (courtesy of Stevenage Museum).*

TWO SISTERS

Services were often conducted by local preachers, stalwarts such as Mr Cox a farmer of Cromer, Mr Aldridge a wheelwright of Walkern, and Mr Raban a saddler of Hitchin. Much of the work of the early church was undertaken by women like the Miss Bardels of Stevenage. BEL provided a sketch of Susan and Becky Bardel for the *Stevenage Argus* of December 1911.

'The two sisters were devotedly attached to each other, but differed very much both in disposition and temperament as well as in appearance. Susan was of medium height, being somewhat proud and haughty, with a genius for interfering. Becky, who was the younger of the two, and a general favourite, was tall and muscular, with two merry black eyes and a dimpled chin, and of a gentle and loving disposition. Becky and her sister were regular attendants at the little old chapel. On Sundays you could have timed your clock twice in the day on seeing them go off to chapel. Becky, with her Bible and Hymn Book held out before her and neatly folded in a clean pocket-handkerchief, looking a picture of happiness. This punctuality was not secured by the possession of a good clock. They had a grandfather clock, but it had stopped going for a long time, and they had to rely upon a form of tallow candle stuck around with pins. It was known as " 'Becky's chapel candle' " or called by her with her slight speech impediment the "tapple tandle". It was always lit on Sunday mornings when a certain express train went by, the pins being so arranged that by the time the candle had burnt down to the first pin it was time for morning service. And so throughout the day they were able, by the exercise of a little patience and ingenuity, to make sure of not being late.'

On the modest gravestone in St Nicholas churchyard, it is recorded of Becky – 'aged 77. She was for sixty years an exemplary member of the Wesleyan Society'.

BEL CULPIN

BEL Culpin retired to live at Battle in Sussex, having been Superintendent of the Sunday School like his father before him, and founding the Bunyan Baptist Church in Basils Road. On the 50th Jubilee of the present Methodist Church in 1927 he wrote a poem for the Revd Leslie Spencer's pamphlet *Wesleyan Methodism in Stevenage*.

DAYS OF THE PAST RETURN

Days of the Past – Return!
Let memory, with her magic Keys, unlock
The years! Then, as each long forgotten scene,
First dim, then clear, appears upon the screen
And old time forms and faces round me flock –
So let the Past return.

The years roll back
To childhood's days – full threescore years and ten;
I am in the old Sunday School – I hear John Moss,
In well-remembered tones, speak of the Cross –
And I'm in Alfred Austin's class again –
As the years roll back.

The years roll back –
It is School-treat day, our goal is Symonds Green;
We cross the old footbridge, a happy throng,
With mugs and waving flags we march along
Until, at last, we reach the festive scene –
So the years roll back.

The years roll back –
It is worship time. Once more I climb the gallery stairs,
Join in the old-time tunes with heart aglow
And watch the folk in high-backed pews below
Close fast the doors and stand and turn at prayers –
As the years roll back.

And how they sang!
With oboe, flute, bass viol and loud bassoon
The singers' voices blend in joyous strain;
'Creation', 'Falcon Street' and old 'Miles Lane',
Ring out again as in the days long gone –
And so they sang.

Before the curtain falls –
I call to mind the worshippers' attire;
The old poke bonnet and the Paisley shawl,
The clogs and pattens and the cloak that covered all –
May be, a heart of gold and a soul on fire,
So let the curtain fall.

THE WESLEYAN METHODIST CHAPEL OF 1876

Fifty or so years before a notice announced preparations for the building of the new chapel.

'Proposed new Wesleyan Chapel and School Rooms at Stevenage – The friends interested in the above scheme are invited to attend a meeting to be held in the Wesleyan Chapel, Stevenage, on Wednesday next, Oct. 21st, 1874. Tea will be provided at 5 o'clock. After the Tea, a Public Meeting will be held, when Addresses will be delivered by the Rev. R. Maxwell (of Bedford), the Circuit Ministers, and other friends. Mr Boyce, of Highgate, is expected to take the chair.'

The Foundation Stone was laid on 27 July, 1876. A photograph of the crowd assembled at the site is reproduced in *Stevenage in Old Photographs*[12]. The ladies wear their Sunday bonnets, the men top hats or Hombergs; many children are clustered towards the front. The old chapel was sold for £177.7.7 pence to Mr Shelford of Stevenage. The cost of the site of the new chapel was £151 – 18 – 6 and the new building (cost £1237.9.8) was opened on 23 November 1876. In 1889 the schoolroom at the east end was enlarged and a new window put in the West end overlooking the main road.

In 1903 the building was renovated, new windows fitted, an organ installed and the interior redecorated through the generosity of Mr J Smart 'whose devotion to the cause found many practical ways of expressing itself, and not least in the inspiration he gave to others by the example of a godly life.' The re-opening was celebrated by a Public Luncheon, tickets two shillings, presided over by the Chairman of the District, supported by the Circuit Stewards and others, 'followed at 6 o'clock by an organ recital by Mr Fred Gostello, F R C O, soloist Mrs Albert Williams. The sister of BEL Culpin, Miss Sarah Barrett Culpin, was at this time Treasurer of the Ladies' Sewing Meeting and survived to attend the Jubilee Celebrations in 1927.

An air of Victorian solemnity pervades the pamphlet *Wesleyan Methodism in Stevenage*. 'Many names could be mentioned of people who did yeoman service (in the interest of Stevenage Methodism)' and 'who, in each generation, contributed to the past glories of our local society'. There was Mr George Barker, 'one of our noble veterans whose passing last December brought sorrow upon us all. By his large-heartedness and sympathetic spirit he won his way into our affections.' As a lay preacher he conducted over 1600 services in various chapels.

And Mrs H J Kingsland: 'The influence of her gracious personality is active in the lives of those among whom she lived and moved.' Simple Anglo-Saxon names like Ayres, Harvey, Miles, Moules, Camfield, Gay and Hawkes, highlighted only here and there by the occasional exotic like the Revd T Jasper Shovell, Junior Minister, who fell in the Great War. By the 1930s, the name of Wallis appears among the officials of the chapel and Stevenage Wesleyan Guild. It may be that about this time the term chapel was dropped in favour of church, although in the programme for the Guild for 1930–31 neither term appears. The Honorary Secretary and Treasurer was my paternal grandfather, Mr W Wallis, his wife a Vice-President, my father Literary Secretary, his sister Miss N Wallis Social Secretary, and my mother, Mrs L Wallis, a member of the Social and Musical Committee. On 12 January 1931, they were to debate 'Are amusements on Sunday justifiable ?'

THE METHODIST CHURCH

The Official Guide to Stevenage of 1946 refers to the Methodist Church in the High Street and a notice of 1954 is issued by the 'Methodist Church, Stevenage and Knebworth Circuit'. What happened to that community of committed and dissenting souls who first banded together to found their own 'chapel'? Perhaps middle-class sensibilities deemed 'a chapel' too reminiscent of early roots amongst labouring men and women. Of course, Primitive Methodists and Strict Baptists still had chapels!

In 1946, Stevenage was taken out of the Hitchin Circuit and, with Knebworth, became the 'Stevenage and Knebworth Methodist Mission' at the behest of the Methodist Conference. This Mission was intended to bring enlightenment to 'Stevenage, old and new, and the surrounding district', with the Revd Donald McNeil as minister.

As a boy, I used to sit with my father in the choir stalls to the left of the pulpit and at right angles to the congregation. Dad sang bass often on his own. Choir numbers in chapels were, I suppose, difficult to sustain in small towns. Ours comprised a tremulous tenor or two, searching for upper notes amongst the rafters, a hawk-nosed soprano and ample contraltos on their cushioned seats in warm, sticky-shellacked pews. The organist could see them when he glanced sideways. He sat embattled behind the pulpit, confronting a battery of stops, pedals and knobs, with a driving mirror above his head so that he could see the preacher. For some months, I earned sixpence a service by pumping the organ to fill the bellows. Five hymns and one psalm when the pressure had to be maintained! Keep the plumbline down lad!

THE COLLECTION

Taking the collection was a slightly surreptitious affair during the penultimate hymn. Offerings were placed inside an all-concealing velvet bag, sometimes as coins, sometimes as small numbered envelopes containing coins or notes. The bag was passed along the row and back to the steward waiting in the aisle. Because my father was Senior Steward, I was able to attend the ritual opening of the bags and envelopes in the vestry; piling coppers, threepenny bits, sixpences, shillings, florins and half-crowns in regular stacks. Half-crowns were good, bank notes thrilling! My father would segregate them all into mysterious, official-looking, paper bank bags. Castles of offerings upon the thick, worn, ink-stained tapestry cloth on the vestry table, all the while scrutinized from the wall by an engraving of John Wesley assessing God's earnings. Scrupulously double-checked, the figures for the morning and the evening collections would be carefully entered in blue-black ink, blotted, and the ledger tenderly closed. Non-conformism needed a healthy credit balance not only in heaven but also at Barclays Bank.

Fig 13 – My father shaking hands with the Revd Donald McNeil in front of the pulpit on his retirement as Circuit Steward. The pulpit was approached by sets of stairs from the right or the left. Also in the photo are, left to right: Harold Perry, Mr Griffiths, Mr Beagrie, Mr Woolner (courtesy of the Herts Pictorial).

SERMONS

Each service was anchored around the sermon. Sometimes these were given by our minister preaching from his commanding turret in the east, pleading, sometimes threatening, shepherd of his flock, exhorter of the weak, cajoler of the strong. How often did he wonder which of his wool-gathering flock had lost the thread? Sundays would often mean an exchange with another minister of the circuit, providing visual if not intellectual variety. Some wore black or charcoal grey and others the ecclesiastical gown and white necktie favoured by John Wesley. On other Sundays we would have a lay-preacher while the Minister 'played away'. These were earnest, admirable, but often uninspiring men, who did their best to disguise the absence of the sacerdotal ingredient. With copious anecdote they would seek to recall their own pathway to enlightenment. Oh, those drowsy hours spent in the brown-shellacked pews in that austere church, bereft of carving and of gothic charm! Oh, for some snake-handling evangelical to declaim: 'Allelujah, Praise the Lord!' Oh, for a Sir Roger de Coverley to rise up and contradict the preacher!

The geometric patterning of the chapel roof beams allowed idle speculation as to whether they were, in engineering terms, a necessity or an extravagance. A reverie upon the climbing tendrils bearing grapes stencilled on the walls in sombre colours suggested they would yield non-alcoholic wine acceptable to chapel folk. Had God, perhaps, mislaid this small insignificant church, foreseen His weakening grip in the forthcoming tide of rampant consumerism?

Methodism for many years was strong for teetotalism and regarded the holding of Premium Bonds as sinful. My dad was able to evade the teetotal police through one of the miracles of modern medicine. Having contracted pneumonia and spent time in hospital, he was sent to a Railway Staff Convalescent Home where the therapeutic regime included half a pint of Guinness a day. Thus, being medicine, Guinness evaded the teetotallers' Rule Book. My dad managed to continue his 'treatment' on his return home. The bottles of dark fluid kept themselves as far out of sight as possible at the back of our cold pantry.

On special days, big-name preachers would come; comfortable men in well-cut suits; men with silver tongues, capable of beguiling us and flattering the ladies. We would get caught up by their stories, persuaded by their arguments almost to the point of conviction. But Wesleyan Methodism kept things low key. No dramatic re-affirmations of faith were usually called for or expected. The state of anaesthesia need not be broken.

Afterwards the guest preachers were provided with 'dinner' or 'lunch' by one of the congregation, depending on their preferred terminology. Out came the best china, the best cutlery and the best manners. The preacher had disarming anecdotes for the nervous family. At the end of every service, the congregation's imminent release was signalled by an ecstatic burst from the organ, perhaps a Bach Toccata to disperse the faithful to their Sunday beanfeasts.

HARVEST FESTIVAL

The church was transformed for Harvest Festival, enriched by flowers, bunches of wheat and sprays of blackberry entwining the brass uprights and pew ends; large vases of Michaelmas daisies, chrysanthemums and dahlias everywhere. This was the time to collect the choicest vegetables, scrub the biggest carrots, spuds, parsnips, beet, find the most perfect apples and pears and set them upon a vast table beneath the pulpit. At the foot of the Communion rail lay pregnant cabbages, replete savoys, blanched cauliflowers, huge swollen marrows and bunches of the reddest carrots. The pulpit, bedecked with sprigs of corn, had attached to its front panel a harvest loaf of platted dough. Each window sill held alternating rows of apples and potatoes with strands of Old Man's Beard twining around them. In the yellow electric light of the Evening Service, the overflowing table glowed with an exuberance alien to drab post-war years. The choir, thin in numbers, struck out with the anthem, a tremulous tenor and two scratchy sopranos announced from their autumnal years that "The valleys stand so thick with corn that they laugh and sing ..."

On the Monday evening an auction of produce was held with a Harvest Supper. In the late forties and early fifties this amounted to plates of salad amid insipid sliced meats or meatloaf, washed down with strong tea or weak fruit squash. Replenishing the vast, enamelled teapots was a task for the Ladies' Guild. The best part of the evening was the auction – an occasion for much jollity – where plates of apples, bunches of carrots, wheat and the Harvest Loaf were held aloft in succession by our affable butcher, who paraded up and down before his audience. The auction was expected to raise a goodly sum for church funds, the bids often greatly exceeding market value. Many items after purchase were donated to the nursing home up the road. The Harvest Loaf with its magnificent crusty ripples was a particularly desirable prize; many a child urged their parents to bid for this centre piece of the harvest display.

SUNDAY SCHOOL

In one corner to the right of the pulpit were some very small seats for the Infants Sunday School, who sang of 'a home for little children above the bright blue sky', the space in which the German bombers used to fly. Gay, unlikely Biblical scenes adorned the walls. Jesus, gentle, serene, distinctly Anglo-Saxon but also hippy, looked down from colour prints. For Sunday School Anniversaries benches were arranged in tiers for children to stand on and uncertain choirs of bashful and grinning infants delivered Sunday School favourites. Prizes 'For the Best Attendance at Sunday School', 'For High Achievement' and so on were presented by the Minister's wife. Perhaps the Sunday School had lost the sense of fun of the Sunday School my mother went to. She and her friends used to sing politically-incorrect, irreligious skits, such as: 'Come join the Darkies' Sunday School and listen to their rhymes', one of whose verses was – as far as I can remember:

> Now Solomon and David lived very wicked lives,
> They went about with dancing girls and other people's wives,
> But later on, or so it's said, they both had serious qualms
> So Solomon wrote the Proverbs and David wrote the Psalms.

And somewhere in the midst of it:

> So God said unto Moses, all men shall have round noses,
> All excepting Aaron, and he shall have a square-un.

SOCIAL ACTIVITIES

In early post-war years there was scant entertainment in Stevenage. Churches sought to capitalise by providing activities for weekday evenings – a 'Womens' Guild', 'The Mens' Fireside', the 'Youth Club'. The Mens' Fireside had a plentiful quota of pensioners, providing billiards, table tennis and darts, as well as more sedate pursuits. The Youth Club directed mild ridicule their way and wouldn't have dreamt of pitting their own superior table tennis skills against them. My father is pictured on one of their coach outings clutching his pipe beside Wilf Piggott, the tenor in our church choir. In the centre of the middle row is Mr Hunt who acted as Harvest Supper auctioneer.

Fig 14 – The 'Mens' Fireside' pictured on an outing in 1955–60. In the second row back, Mr Piggott is on the far right standing beside my father. Directly behind them is the Revd Donald McNeil. Seated far left is Harold Perry with Mr Beagrie, third from left and crouching.

The Stevenage and Knebworth Mission raised further building funds in the expanded circuit by holding a large auction on 4 June 1949 on Mr Lines' field in Pound Avenue. New Buildings had been erected at Knebworth on 9 April 1949 and at Oaklands, Welwyn later in the month. In 1948 the men of the circuit had put up a wooden building at Broadwater, part of Stevenage New Town, and the year before had converted a garage into a Sunday School before starting building the church.

Items for auction ranged from a football autographed by the Tottenham Hotspur team and another one autographed by Leicester City while staying in Stevenage on the eve of the Cup Final and by Wolves, the

Cup winners, to live calves, pigs and cockerels. A silver egg-timer was the lot preceding a cricket bat used by C B Fry in a Gents versus Players match at Lords, where he made 232 not out. Several half-hundredweights of chicken corn appeared as lots before a 'china Scottish soldier, a really lovely doll' and two infant chairs, 8 inches high. The support of several local farmers was reflected in the livestock items – one cross-bred Hereford calf, one Wessex-cross Large White store pig, one 5 month-old pure-bred Large Black gilt, six pure Rhode-Island-Red pullets, three 5 month-old cockerels, one trussed boiling fowl and, finally, six cucumbers, two polo mallets and a lacrosse racquet!

4

Fairview Road – War Time

Fairview Road was long and straight with a gravel and tar surface and uneven pavements. Where the curbs are now were narrow grass verges abutting sandy gutters. The road was quiet in 1940 and the gutters well-suited to games of marbles. You could scoop out a sandy hollow into which 'to hole' your marble. Glass marbles with coloured whirls, 'gob-stoppers' and metal ball-bearings were all used for games.

A good many farm carts pulled by horses used Fairview Road, carrying swedes, sugar-beet, straw, corn or manure. Eager gardeners, especially if they worked an allotment, were keen to apply any horse dung to their plots. Either you went out yourself with bucket and spade to collect Nature's Bounty or you persuaded some idiot boy to do it for you. I became an accomplished, not to say avid, collector of horse dung!

At its northern end Fairview Road veered slightly eastwards towards the railway station. Here the Educational Supply Association – the ESA – had a factory and extensive yards and sheds for drying and seasoning wood. Some of the largest sheds were close to the main railway line. A conflagration in these woodyards was to provide the inhabitants of Fairview Road with the most exciting spectacle of these years. What started the fire or exactly when it happened I'm not sure, but numerous appliances were defeated by the swirling leaping flames and cascading columns of sparks as the fire spread both sides of the road. The woodworking expertise of the ESA was harnessed during the war to the fabrication of the wooden wings for De Havilland Mosquito fighter-bombers. The painted wings complete with roundels could be seen standing around or leaving the factory on transporter lorries.

Illness and Recovery

Dad joined the Home Guard on 6 August 1941. The year before he had been seriously ill with pneumonia and taken to hospital in Hertford. A bad cold in early January during a spell of intensely cold weather quickly led to pleurisy. On 22 January 1940, mum's diary tells of the stopcock being frozen. Three days later Dad was taken to Hertford by ambulance and remained there until 27 March. During those anxious weeks his condition first deteriorated. The diary says: 'Len looked rotten. Scared me stiff.' What the treatment was I do not know. Possibly just good nursing, because antibiotics would not then have been available. Mum made trips to see him by train, by bus and by hire car, although for a part of this time the buses do not appear to have been running. The diary entry for 27 March is: 'Len fetched home in Mrs Males' car. Very pleased to have him back.' His recovery continued to be slow and a period in a Railway Convalescent Home was deemed advisable. Dad went to the Par Convalescent Home on 18 April and stayed there until 2 May 1940.

AIR RAIDS AND SOLDIERS

1940 had been a year of increasing but minor military activity in Stevenage. Mum's diary records in a low key way day-to-day events in a Stevenage scarcely ruffled by the air war over Southern England. Stray German bombers, however, sometimes used the main railway line North as a guide to the East coast, and occasionally jettisoned their load of bombs. The diary records mum attending First Aid lectures. On 10 May a gas mask was obtained for Graham, my younger brother aged just two. On 29 May soldiers arrived in Fairview Road. On 6 June, one was brought home to tea. This was Colin Legerton, who 'seemed very nice', stayed with us until 12 June and on his departure presented mum with a box of Black Magic chocolates. Had he been at Dunkirk? Chocolates of any sort were virtually unobtainable for most of the war.

On 31 July, 'sand arrived', in August there were frequent air-raid warnings and on 3 September: 'Bombs were dropped at the end of the road behind farm.' My dad was still going by train to work in London. The diary says for 7 September 1940: 'Terrific air-raids over London – E End gets it badly' and on 9 September 'Len back at office. Very worrying cos of all day raids.' Life went on, however, and blackberries needed picking. On 21 September 1940: 'Len to work in morning – office got bashed so home by 1.45 pm. Dora and I went blackberrying. Got stung on the foot by wasp. Got over 2 lbs.' Dora was the Evacuee and something of a horror. She sulked and cried, had tantrums, soiled her bed, poor thing, and set off at least once to find her way back to London. '30 May, 1942: Dora didn't come back after a visit to London. Monday 1 June: Dora arrived at 10.10pm. Little d----.'

The Queen with great magnanimity sent us a cyclostyled letter some time after the war as follows:

> I wish to mark, by this personal message, my appreciation of the service you have rendered to your Country in 1939.
>
> In the early days of the War you opened your door to strangers who were in need of shelter, & offered to share your home with them. I know that to this unselfish task you have

sacrificed much of your comfort, & that it could not have been achieved without the loyal co-operation of all in your household. By your sympathy you have earned the gratitude of those to whom you have shown hospitality, & by your readiness to serve you have helped the State in a work of great value.

Elizabeth R

Mrs Wallace [sic]

On 27 September, a land-mine exploded in the fields behind the house. The diary says: 'Very unsettling – Air-raid warnings all night'. For the first air-raid or two, we all clustered in the tiny cupboard under the stairs until the all-clear sounded. Some families – not ours – had acquired Anderson Shelters and erected them in their gardens. Under the stairs was good enough for us, at least for two air-raids, but the discomfort and cramps induced soon seemed more of a risk than staying comfortably in bed and relying on the Germans to miss. In any case, my bed was soon moved downstairs to the cold sitting room in the front of the house and a bed for Dora was made up on the sofa. Black-out material was bought from Blows the Drapers on 19 October. The crater made by the land-mine was a local tourist attraction, providing a focal point for country walks for several weeks afterwards.

MR WHITTON

People were still moving from London to safer havens such as Stevenage. On 10 October a Mr Whitton called about a room. The diary records: 'Fixed up if Len agreeable.' Mr Whitton stayed with us, on and off, until 3 May 1941. He was a business man, apparently comfortably off and comfortably padded. Affable and avuncular, on his return from business trips he would often present me with a small bar of chocolate. He had a penchant for hot buttered toast with lots of butter. My father watched the consumption of this toast with some alarm, and muttered to himself in the kitchen, as butter was strictly rationed with a relatively small amount allowed per person. Mr Whitton appeared in danger of eating not only his own ration but everyone else's as well. My mother mentions him rarely in the diary, but when she does, it is often in connection with him having just managed to catch the train or she notes disparagingly his tardiness on Saturday mornings. The railway station was then at the north end of Fairview Road and survived largely unscathed until the 1970s, as shown in the drawing. On 9 November, the diary records: 'Mr Whitton stayed in bed till 12.' Living in our house in 1940 was for me, and even more for Mr Whitton, a spartan experience. By 1941 he had acquired a fiancée and

If I were a Blackbird ...

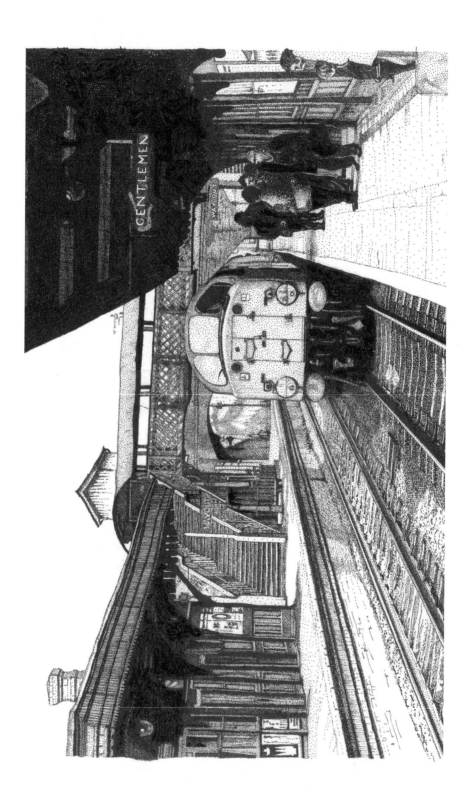

Fig 15 – Old Stevenage Railway Station in 1973. Drawing from a photograph in Stevenage in Old Photographs. *Service on the line to London was no better in 1950 than it had been in 1884. In June 1884 there were eleven trains daily from Stevenage to King's Cross, the slowest of which took 75 and the fastest 50 minutes for the 30-mile journey. By June 1950 the number of trains had increased to 23, but the slowest took 92 and the fastest 49 minutes. Deterioration in rail services was widespread through Britain* (The Times, *9 Jan 1950). A letter to the press from an irate commuter stated that ' service has so deteriorated that passengers are beside themselves with joy when they arrive at work or home only five minutes late instead of twenty-five, thanks to the Late and Never Early Railway' (the LNER which served London and the East Coast).*

In December 1949 the total commuting population of Stevenage was some 9 – 12% of the total employed population (estimated as around 400 people, 175 of whom travelled on reduced-daily workman tickets).

the prospect of a more comfortable existence. He called with her on August 3rd 1941, had tea, then – the diary says – 'packed up, finished with room.'

A weekly shopping bill for 1940 records a total expenditure of £1.15s.3d, involving: Jones (grocers) 7s, milk 6s, bread 3s, meat 4s 6d, papers 1s 6d, insurance 1s 8d, coal 2s, bacon 3s, fish 1s 10d, cakes 1s 2d, eggs 1s 7d and veg 2s.

EVACUEES

Stevenage during the war was host to some two thousand evacuated Londoners and workers directed by the Government to nearby factories or farms and billeted in local homes. Harold Orlans[10] remarks that 'the enforced contact between lower-class visitors and middle-class natives led to unfortunate episodes and much ill-feeling on both sides'. A Labour Councillor declared in 1941 that 'at the top end of the housing scale people with rooms to spare have shirked taking in evacuees, but now are taking in people able and willing to pay rents which are definitely exorbitant'. Needless to say, he was not referring to 98 Fairview Road. According to Orlans, – some workers found themselves locked out if they got in late in the evening. 'Local citizens complained that lodgers were often dirty, smelly, noisy, troublesome and dissatisfied with life in a small town; and the Londoners had complaints of their own. The simple truth was that class differences in attitudes and behaviour, in many cases, were too great to be ignored or peacefully overcome.' These wartime experiences, Orlans notes, were remembered a few years later when the New Town project was broached, and middle-class opposition was conditioned, in part, by the wish to avoid a new influx of working-class

Londoners. Significantly, Stevenage Town Council approved the Greater London Plan but with the proviso that attention be paid to obtaining a 'balanced population', a euphemism for a substantial proportion of middle-class relative to working-class residences and houses[10].

DAD AND THE HOME GUARD

My dad was friendly with Mr Bickell, the local watch and clock repairer – '8 day striking clocks from £4.19s.6d' in 1949. His son Richard was one of my friends. When the Home Guard issued dad with a formidably large and cumbersome 303 rifle, where else would he take it to be cleaned up? The diary for 8 November 1941 notes: 'Len and David went to Bickell's to clean up rifle.' Frequent parades are recorded; on 27 August 'Len has got a tin hat' and on 17 September 'his uniform.' Dad served in the Home Guard until 31 December 1944. The most draining part of it was the all-night guard duties. He was drafted into the Signal Section and eventually made a Corporal, guided by his mentor, Bunny Ashman.

After the war, the grateful nation rewarded him with a cyclostyled letter signed George R I, reproduced below.

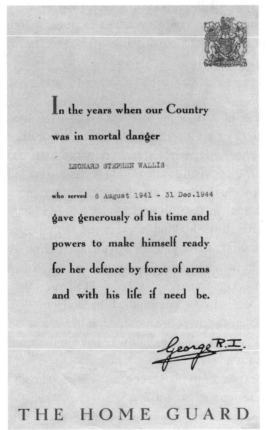

In truth, things were often shambolic and a better sense of what was achieved, and against what odds, is suggested by the letter from the commander of the Signal Section, Lieutenant 'Bunny' Ashman. Dated 7 December 1944 and addressed to Cpl L Wallis, Signal Section, No 2C Company it reads:

Fig 16 – Cyclostyled certificate to Home Guard Volunteers from King George VI

TO ALL MEMBERS OF THE SIGNAL SECTION

HOME GUARD 'STAND DOWN'

With the "Stand Down" parade of the 2nd Bn. Herts. H.G. now behind us, the time seems appropriate for me to send a word of thanks to the Signal Section, though the final farewell is for the moment not yet in sight.

Since its formation in August 1940, the Section has done a first class job of work, and has achieved a reputation of which we may all be justly proud. Hampered till the last by lack of the proper tools, we have justified the British reputation for improvisation, whilst painfully aware all the time of the limitations it imposed. By unending toil and patience we surmounted our disadvantages, and at all times provided communications which were more than adequate to requirements. Indeed, it would be true to say that at times the standard of our work showed up the shortcomings of those originating the messages.

We can therefore rest content that the compliments paid to us were well and truly earned. Linemen patrolled miles of cable in all weathers and kept us in touch, whilst the Signal Office staff, operators and clerks, were at all times on their toes and kept the wires humming. The volume of message traffic during exercises was extraordinary, and the percentage of errors quite insignificant.

During the special duties associated with "D"–Day, work was particularly arduous, involving long hours of strain and concentration. The standard set by the Section at that time afforded me great personal satisfaction, and was a real reward for my own efforts.

It but remains to express my gratitude for your devoted and loyal service. Signallers have always been a fraternity of kindred spirits bound together by the nature of their job, and our Section has displayed this feeling in full measure.

To you all, from the humble private who carried the ladder and humped the drum, to the N.C.O.'s who gave me helpful counsel and loyal support at all times, I send my greetings and thanks, and I assure you this chapter in our lives will always have a special niche in my remembrance. If I couple with this a special word of regard for our Sergeant, who has been friend and comrade to us all, I know I shall be expressing the feelings of everyone.

"Stand down" it is, then, chaps. Greetings and Adieu.

B L Ashman
Lieut.

Fig 17 – My father's Home Guard Signal Platoon in about 1942. My father is sitting on the far left of the front row holding a flag, next to Lieutenant 'Bunny' Ashman.

BUNNY ASHMAN'S HOUSE

Bunny Ashman lived further down Fairview Road and was a technological whizz. Near to the house he had a workshop in which he constructed in brass working model steam engines. Shelves were lined with burnished parts of engines gleaming purposefully amongst various sets of tools. With his son Alan he showed me how to work a 'Cat's Whisker' radio receiver. In his back garden were further delights. Straddling the garden half-way down was a series of small concrete streams, ponds and culverts, with bridges here and there, over which wended a model railway line passing though a rockery. Unfortunately I never enjoyed the thrill of seeing steam engines in action pulling a train along the Rock Island Line. Alan would take me to the end of the garden which was pure clay, and not far from the clay brickfield adjacent to the railway line near Chequers Road. Trow-Smith – talks of the 'cold clays of northern Hertfordshire, legacies of the Ice Age ... intractable to the man with the plough.' He envisaged hunters and fugitives losing their implements and weapons as they passed through or camped nearby, in these inhospitable clay lands which still bore 'their primaeval cover of oak and elm and ash.' In fact, the brickfields have yielded a store of paleolithic flints.

The clay was ideal for children digging trenches and constructing shelters, as Alan had done in his back garden, as well as for fashioning their own primitive weapons in the form of baked clay pellets. These we hurled with less than benign intent but faulty aim at children we perceived as the current enemy. The smoking of tobacco then – perhaps less so now – was an adult vice infinitely attractive to us. It was easy to purchase the old style clay pipes from the High Street into which the pickings from collected cigarette ends could be stuffed and smoked! The clay trench-cum-shelter provided excellent cover and the benign Mr. Ashman never bothered his son or his friend to find out what was going on in their den. Slips of newspaper could also be rolled up to form cigarettes and filled with the same disgusting detritus of discarded fag ends. When these ran out, we tried on more than one occasion the even more dreadful expedient of twists of oily rag which Bunny Ashman's shed furnished in abundance. Mercifully children soon get bored with things!

CONVOYS AND VE DAY

In 1941, and at various times during the war, a host of army lorries appeared in Fairview Road. In July 1941 soldiers came in for tea and on 21 November two soldiers came in for a wash and shave so the diary records. Convoys appeared in the road several times during 1943 and 1944. All this led up to the diary recording for 7 May 1945: 'News of German surrender expected any minute – Great excitement – Tomorrow's V E day – Holiday – Lovely weather'; and for 8 May: 'V.E. Day – Germans unconditionally surrendered – everyone full of it – I went up to London – Len and I in garden – saw lights up down Street at 11.15pm – boys had lovely bonfire – Went to Thanksgiving Service in Benington.' And eventually on 14 August 1945: 'News very good – Lots of rumours.' 15 August: 'V J Day – News of holiday on 7 o'clock News – great excitement – decided to have party tomorrow – bonfire and fireworks at night.' 16 August: 'Very busy getting ready for party – had it outside in road – children had a very good time – sports in field afterwards.'

Long trestle tables were erected in Fairview Road and all of us feasted on jellies, blancmanges, sandwiches and cakes all hastily knocked up for the occasion, jugs of squash and homemade lemonade quenched our thirst, the sun shone and no one mentioned atom bombs or Belsen or Hiroshima.

If I were a Blackbird ...

Fig 18 – The Wallis brothers in the back garden of 98 Fairview Road in 1942. Graham is sitting in the car and the author is sitting on the bonnet. Protective tape to stop window glass fragmenting into the house can be seen on the upstairs' windows.

Fig 19 – The garden of 98 Fairview Road in the 1970s. The adjacent house to the right with the shed belonged to our neighbours, George and Doris Hinton.

5

FAIRVIEW ROAD AND THE NEW TOWN

A PIG IN A POKE, MR IRETON

One drama was still to come for Fairview Road. Under the New Towns Act of August 1946 of the post-war Attlee Government, the area of Stevenage west of the Great North Road and the LNER main line railway would be an industrial zone, while areas to the east would be residential. All houses of the one hundred or so in Fairview Road would be subject to compulsory purchase and demolished. The subsequent protests led to a meeting in the Town Hall, where the Minister of Housing, Lewis Silkin, was booed, abused and pelted with over-ripe tomatoes. The tyres of the ministerial car were deflated as feelings inflated and sand was put into the petrol tank. Mr Presland from over the road asked how he could be

Fig 20 – 'Practice with a stirrup pump, Second World War' – Mr Presland of Fairview Road, with pipe, looks on in a carefully posed picture to publicize the use of the stirrup pump. Our neighbour, Doris Hinton (working the pump on the right), no doubt selected by the photographer because of her and her friend's photogenic qualities, demonstrates how to push the plunger. My Aunt Nellie (second from right), my dad's sister who lived in nearby Bridge Road, had somehow learnt of the photo opportunity and arrived in her Sunday best complete with hat. (photo from Stevenage Voices*)*

compensated for his dozen mature fruit trees. A meeting held further down the road near the junction with Bury Mead comprised a host of householders fervently opposed to the scheme. Standing separately, a few yards away, a small knot of people clustered around Mr Phil Ireton. Mr Ireton, a Labour Councillor, was a supporter of the plan but also a resident of Fairview Road. The meeting ended with Mr Berry shouting out, having attempted to orchestrate our protests: 'You are buying a pig in a poke, Mr Ireton.'

Orlans in his 1952 book *Stevenage, A Sociological Study of a New Town*[10] provides a fuller account of the conversation between Mr Silkin and Mr Presland, although Orlans refers to the latter as Mr T. The Ministerial car was touring Fairview Road and stopped half-way along. The car had passed people bearing posters saying: 'Hands off Our Homes' and 'NO! NO! Mr Minister'. An elderly man approached Mr Silkin, who said, 'Is there anything you want to ask me ?' Mr Presland invited him to tour his garden. 'When have we got to move ? Are you going to turn us out ?'

Silkin: 'You are not going to be turned out. You will never be asked to move until there is somewhere for you to go. We shall build you another home.'

A lady, perhaps Mrs Presland, interpolated: 'It won't be prefabs ?'

Minister: 'No, it won't be prefabs'.

Lady: 'But we may run on for years, worrying whether we shall be turned out or not. We don't want another house. We want this one.'

Mr Presland, placing his hand on Silkin's shoulder and pointing to an apple tree laden with blossom: 'Can you put in a tree like that? It is twenty years old. You can't give me back my fruit trees!'

Minister: 'No, that is true.'

Lady: 'We are too late in life to start a new home'.

A crowd of newspapermen had surged up the garden path, one entering the house to take photographs out of a bedroom window and another, quipping to a local resident: 'And this is the nationalised strawberry bed'.

The New Towns Act provided for the development of new self-contained towns by public corporations appointed by the Minister of Town and Country Planning and financed by the Treasury. It implemented, in varying degrees, recommendations of (i) the Barlow Report to Neville Chamberlain's Coalition Government in 1939, calling for decentralization of the nation's industry and population; (ii) Professor Abercrombie's Greater London Plan of 1944 prepared for Herbert Morrison, then Minister of Town and Country Planning, which proposed the relocation of over a million people from central London to a ring of new satellite towns and expanded old towns; and of (iii) the Reith Committee reports of 1946 which gave advice on the way New Towns should be developed. Stevenage, population 6,500, was designated in November 1946 as the site of the first New Town. It was to draw inhabitants from over-crowded areas of London to achieve a population of 60,000. Orlans[10] quotes a local resident as saying: 'It's all because Abercrombie put his finger on a map. And he probably never even saw it.'

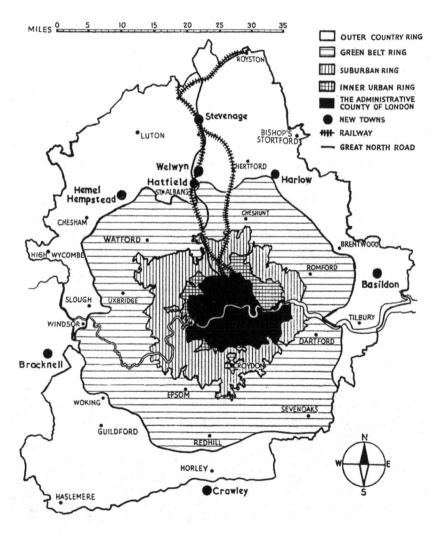

Fig 21 – Greater London Plan – Amended from the Greater London Plan 1944, *Patrick Abercrombie, showing the Four Rings. Of the eight New Town sites indicated, only Stevenage and Harlow were recommended in the Plan; the others were chosen subsequently.*

If I were a Blackbird ...

PLANNERS AND PLANNEES

Orlans' book[10] is a readable, critical analysis of the conflicts and tensions which arose between the rival groups – the planners and the planned upon, the Ministry, the Development Corporation, Stevenage Council and Stevenage residents. In particular, he clarifies how the decision to demolish Fairview Road came about and how alternative schemes proposed by the Council sought to modify or even thwart the Master Plan. Most details that follow have been gleaned from his book, which arose from interviewing, observation and documentary research conducted over an eighteen-month period from October, 1948.

STEVENAGE U D C AND THE DEVELOPMENT CORPORATION

Several factors seemed to have set Stevenage Urban District Council and the Development Corporation, backed by the Ministry, at loggerheads.

First, the Ministry had decided to make Stevenage the first Satellite Town, establish a Development Corporation and begin building before the New Towns Act had been approved by Parliament. They were able to make use of a provision of the Town and Country Planning Act of 1932 under the terms of which the Minister had requested the county (Hertfordshire), as agents of the Ministry, to purchase immediately and, if necessary, compulsorily, 5,500 acres of land including the whole of the Stevenage Urban District except for the built up area.

Secondly, Stevenage Council had itself suggested the development of the town before the war. In October 1937 its plan for Stevenage anticipated growth to a population of 34,000 and an industrial zone west of the railway but south of Fairview Road. In fact in 1946 the Minister had asked his officials whether it would not be possible to plan the New Town on the basis of the Council's 1937 proposals. But the Council's Plan was hurriedly devised to satisfy local needs and mainly perpetuated existing land use. It was not in any way a blueprint for a New Town and could not easily be expanded to accommodate 60,000 without extending considerably to the north and the further side of a planned east-to-west arterial road. Orlans reports the Minister as finding the Council's 1937 Plan 'offends against many of the canons of good planning.'

Although the Council's initial responses to the Abercrombie Plan's proposal of Stevenage as the first New Town were relatively favourable, they subsequently felt that their views were not receiving an adequate hearing. The Council had seen an advance copy of the Plan in December 1944. Their Town Planning and Development Committee recommended 'that the proposal to site a satellite town at Stevenage be approved in principle subject to reservations with regard to financial provisions and any necessary boundary revisions.' This Committee visited the Ministry's offices in London in June 1945 for discussions. Orlans notes that these preliminary approaches were often forgotten in later months; many Stevenage residents were hardly aware they had taken place. As the war was not over until August 1945 and the Labour landslide election victory did not occur until July of that year, perhaps this is not surprising.

OPPOSITION TO THE PLAN

In October 1945 Ministry officials twice visited the Council Offices to inform it that the Ministry intended to start work immediately on a master plan. The *Hertfordshire Express* learned about the clause in the 1932 Town and Country Planning Act for compulsory purchase of land in Stevenage. The newspaper coverage evoked letters of protest and the Council's Town Planning Committee, meeting late into the night, resolved 'to recommend that the Minister of Town and Country Planning should be asked to send representatives to meet the whole of the Council on this question ...and that the Ministry be informed that the Council wish in future to be informed directly of developments.'

Subsequently, leaks from the Ministry and disclosures from the Council led to Ministry officials becoming even more cautious about confiding in the Council. Although confidential plans showing the layout of the proposed New Town were shown to Council representatives, most news came from private sources or after the event. Even staunch Labour Councillors began to complain about the Ministry's lack of co-operation. The Council was often asked for information and was sometimes retrospectively advised of developments, but it was seldom consulted on an equal footing during planning. At a public meeting at which F J Osborn, chairman of the Town and Country Planning Association and a member of the Reith Committee, talked to the subject 'New Towns', he was asked what action the Ministry would take if the residents of Stevenage voted against the plan. He answered that this was a democratic country, and their views would have weight if there was sound reason behind them, but, if it were in the interests of Greater London, the town would be built in Stevenage whether they wanted it or not[15].

LETTER TO FAIRVIEW ROAD RESIDENTS

In April, Ministry officers presented a draft plan to Stevenage Council and promised to consult the Council more frequently in the future. Simultaneously the occupants of Fairview Road received letters marked OHMS and stamped Ministry of Town and Country Planning, which set out terms and conditions for acquiring, either by agreement or compulsorily, the land 'of which it is understood you are the freehold owner.' By concluding agreement the owner was liable to eviction upon three months' notice. The Council had received no prior notification of this letter and most of them felt betrayed. Fairview Road residents were outraged. A local businessman, who had already written letters of protest to the press, asked twelve friends to his house so that a Residents' Protection Association might be set up. Once established it grew rapidly to claim 1200 members.

The visit of the Minister to Stevenage occurred on 6 May only a few days after a large coloured plan of the New Town had been posted in shop windows in the High Street. This had attracted immediate attention, a crowd collecting and clusters of people poring over the map all day and late into the evening. Council Officials were continually pestered with queries during the day and police were on hand to shepherd the crowds and protect the Minister. His Wolseley arrived at 1 pm to be besieged by reporters. He walked to the Council Chamber under a battery of cameras. The meeting with the Town Council was followed by a tour of the town in a convoy consisting of a police car, the Minister's Wolseley and twenty cars full of camera men and reporters.

THE PUBLIC MEETING

Four hours before the public meeting in the Town Hall was to begin, a queue had formed stretching round the corner and down the High Street. Music was relayed over loudspeakers to carry the Minister's speech to a crowd some thousands strong – the Town Hall held only three to four hundred. A multitude of cars contributed to the general hubbub and cheers and boos greeted the Minister as he made his way up to the platform in the Town Hall. The meeting was opened by the Council Chairman who was a stalwart supporter of the New Town.

'This is a great day for Stevenage,' he began, but the rest of the sentence was lost in hoots of laughter, catcalls and general uproar. When the Minister rose the hubbub returned. He managed to quieten the crowd by insisting he would not shout and would not speak unless people would listen. In a cogent speech which Orlans reproduces almost in its entirety, Lewis Silkin explained the planning decisions that led to Stevenage being chosen.

'I propose to tell you ... why Stevenage was recommended by Sir Patrick Abercrombie and approved by the Government. I will then deal with the objections which have been brought to my notice, and finally I will tell you a little about the plans and proposals we have in mind for Stevenage, the kind of town we want to build, and what it will mean to Stevenage. He went on to compare the Ministry's plan with the previous Town Council plans to enlarge to 30,000. He pointed out that change was inevitable. Stevenage had changed between the wars from a built up area confined largely to the High Street and a few roads running from it to a town straggling over a mile or more in many directions, providing one of the very bad examples of ribbon development.'

'The Council's Plan', he asserted, 'divides the residential population in two by means of the railway, which many of you will no doubt know is one of the main defects of Welwyn Garden City. In order to preserve a number of small houses,' – he was referring to Fairview Road – 'factories are to be built on both sides of the row of houses when clearly the most convenient place of industry is the whole of the area between the main road' – the planned A1 (M) to the west – 'and the railway ... The Council's plan would in fact necessitate the dispossession of nearly as many people as the New Town Plan.' (The Council Chairman had already pointed out that the Council scheme involved re-development, according to one source, the demolition of the whole of the High Street), 'but, even though every organisation in the town was circularised, no one objected. Every organisation was consulted and no one replied.'

The Minister went on to outline the broad proposals of the Master Plan, which created a new town centre just to the south of the existing one and moved the railway station a mile or two south to be more conveniently situated for the new centre. 'I want to carry out in Stevenage a daring exercise in town planning (Jeers!). It is no good your jeering: it is going to be done (Applause and boos. Cries of 'Dictator!'). The authoritarian tone was mixed with a somewhat utopian vision. "One of the things which is most lacking in our present day towns ... but which is still retained in villages, is the spirit of friendliness and neighbourliness ... I should like somehow so to build our New Town that this neighbourly, friendly

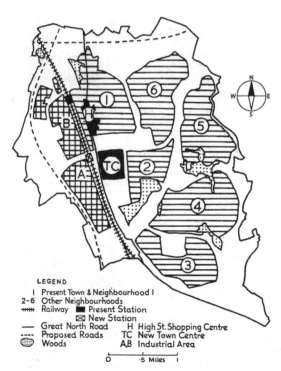

LEGEND
I   Present Town & Neighbourhood I
2-6 Other Neighbourhoods
━━ Railway   ■ Present Station
      ⊠ New Station
—   Great North Road   H High St.Shopping Centre
---- Proposed Roads   TC New Town Centre
⬡ Woods   A,B Industrial Area

0   ·5 Miles

Fig 22 – Stevenage New Town Master Plan, 1950 –
(Orlans[10])

social spirit is not lost.' There might be 'neighbourhood units containing perhaps a nursery school, a communal kitchen and restaurant, and a small community centre. In the communal kitchen food would be prepared by a rota of women living in the units ... I want the new towns to be beautiful. I am a firm believer in the cultural and spiritual influence of beauty.' Finally, he asked for co-operation and appealed to their community spirit.

THE REFERENDUM

Later in May 1946, the Council held a referendum asking voters to select one of three options:

1. I am in favour of the scheme for a satellite town at Stevenage as outlined by the Ministry of Town and Country Planning.

2. I am in favour of the scheme as outlined by the Ministry subject to a substantial reduction in the number of houses to be demolished and other modifications to be submitted by the Council. Also subject to compensation being paid to all owners of land and property upon the basis of the market value at the date of acquisition by the Ministry, and comparable accommodation, with payment of removal and incidental expenses, being offered to all displaced families.

3. I am entirely against the siting of a satellite town at Stevenage.

The Residents' Protection Association held meetings in the town hall and conducted a vigorous campaign to canvas votes for proposal 3; proposal 2 was termed a 'trap'. A public enquiry was demanded. The Association chairman declared: 'We imagined tyranny was dead, but now I feel that a different sort of tyranny is still abroad – the tyranny of the acquisition of houses and lands, and the tyranny of control from Whitehall over homes.' No propaganda was conducted in favour of the New Town. It was expected that the opposition to the scheme would win an overwhelming victory for proposal 3, even though Labour Councillors had mixed sympathies about the plan. Independent Councillors, Conservatives in disguise, were firmly against it. The results surprised many people. *The Times*[16] had suggested proposal 2 would win a majority, for instance. Proposal 2 gained only 11% of votes, proposal 1 as many as 36.5% and proposal 3 52.5%.

The Council next informed the Ministry that it objected to the siting of the new town at Stevenage; the latter replied on 14 June that, while due weight was certainly attached to the views of the electors of Stevenage, a referendum which reflected their views alone must necessarily be of limited significance in relation to such a matter as the siting of the proposed New Town.

In August, the Minister published a draft order designating Stevenage as the site of the New Town and appointed an Advisory Committee which later became the Stevenage Development Corporation to lay the groundwork for development.

Persons unknown altered the platform sign at Stevenage station to read SILKINGRAD!

THE RESIDENTS' PROTECTION ASSOCIATION RESORTS TO LAW

In October 1946, a public inquiry was held at Stevenage Town Hall and various objections laid before a Ministry inspector by the Residents' Protection Association, the local branch of the National Farmers' Union, Stevenage Council and others. No witnesses appeared for the Ministry, so opponents were hopeful that the scheme might be abandoned. But on 11 November the Minister confirmed the Stevenage New Town (Designation) Order and on 5 December the Stevenage Development Corporation was formed from the Advisory Committee.

The Town Council was not resolutely opposed to the New Town. A Labour Councillor proposed that they 'co-operate conscientiously in the successful building of the New Town,' providing the Minister reconsider the demolition of the houses; he believed most citizens would agree with such a decision, despite the results of a referendum 'decided by the loudspeaker vans and motor-cars of the opposition.' Four Labour and two Independents voted for and six Independents against the motion, which was carried by the chairman's casting vote. Nevertheless, the Minister refused to receive a delegation from the Council, whose Chairman complained that 'the way we have been treated is abominable.'

The Residents' Protection Association, represented by three people including Farmer W V Franklin of Rooks Nest together with the National Farmers' Union, next brought an action in the High Court to have the Designation Order annulled on the grounds that the Minister, having shown himself biased (notably in the town hall address of May) had not fairly considered objections entered at the public inquiry. Justice Henn Collins heard the case in the King's Bench Division on 10 and 11 February 1947, and quashed the Order on Feb 20th. 'I am convinced,' he ruled, 'that the Minister did not consider the question: "Aye or No should the Order be confirmed?" with an open mind, but that he meant to confirm it whatever the force of the objections might be ... This involves a denial of natural justice ... ' The judgement was overturned on appeal as early as the next month. The Court of Appeal held that even if the Minister was biased in May, it had not been proved he remained biased while fulfilling his duties in regard to the inquiry.

The Residents' Protection Association launched a campaign to carry the fight to the House of Lords, having run through their funds. Three thousand pounds was needed to take the case to the Lords. A town hall crowd was asked to remember the little man who was here that night and said 'You are going to have the scheme whether you like it or not.' 'In England, people will not tolerate such dictation ... and it filled us with a sense of burning injustice.' A leaflet called: 'The Battle of Stevenage' was widely distributed. It stated that 'inevitable chaos ... must result if Stevenage, this gracious old Market Town with roots in the fifteenth century, is crucified on the cross of progress.' The fight over the town was 'David and Goliath all over again: the small men against the powerful bureaucratic machine.'

Although the Development Corporation regarded themselves as hindered by the continuing legal action, on 24 July 1947 the House of Lords upheld the Minister's Order. Five Law Lords were unanimous that questions of justice and Ministerial bias – *ie* the right under English natural justice to a hearing before an impartial judge (the Minister) – were completely irrelevant to the case, because the Minister was acting throughout in an administrative and not a judicial or quasi-judicial capacity.

Stevenage was predominantly rural and conservative. It might have been predicted that there would be opposition to a scheme which threatened to raise rates, abolish private ownership of land and homes, put many farmers out of business and change the character of the district. Some opponents of the scheme tactlessly asserted that, where interests diverged, the welfare of the majority should yield to the minority (*ie* houseless Londoners yield to local residents). But, as Orlans[10] concludes, 'no matter how selfish the motives, opponents performed a distinct public service by subjecting the actions of the Ministry and the Development Corporation to the scrutiny of the courts, Ministerial tribunals, and national opinion, revealing very real problems and dangers therein, which New Town enthusiasts were inclined to overlook.'

THE TREASURY STEPS IN

A national economic crisis delayed progress on the New Town and in August 1947 the Treasury forbade the Corporation to enter into any contracts. Sir Stafford Cripps told Parliament that 'Work on the new towns during the coming year will, in general, be limited to the provision of basic services ... '. The *Hertfordshire Mercury* described the Corporation 'living a somewhat worried existence ... with an imminent "Government axe" hanging over their heads. Everyone expects that within the next ten days a Ministerial announcement will decide ... whether it will go forward according to plan ... or be relegated to the limbo of ... increasingly forgotten projects.' The *New Statesman*, adapting Oliver Goldsmith, published 'The Deserted Satellite':

> 'Sweet Stevenage! Loveliest township ever planned,
> Before the dollar crisis stripp'd the land,
> Who could, unmov'd, trace thy forsaken sites,
> Fairest of London's stillborn satellites?

The building programme for the New Town was revised, and revised again, as bureaucratic manoeuvres by the local opposition were added to the prolonged national economic difficulties. By 1948, two years after its establishment, the Development Corporation had erected a total housing stock of 20 prefabricated bungalows. These were for Corporation staff, for not a single dwelling had been built for Londoners.

Further delays and alterations ensued, together with a second public inquiry held in October 1949. The Master Plan for the New Town was approved by the Minister in February 1950, a year before the first London family moved to a new home in Stevenage. Fairview Road was still in a designated industrial area. Relations between the Development Corporation and Stevenage Council began to improve; it was agreed that the plan for the re-development of old Stevenage would be prepared jointly. But throughout three years of discussion the Corporation stuck firmly with the demolition of Fairview Road, although conceding that this development could be delayed until a later stage of the programme.

The Ministry and Corporation were not blind to the Council's alternative schemes, but their main obligation was to prepare as good a scheme as geographic, economic, agricultural and engineering considerations allowed. They would not sanction a proposal which, they felt, might produce the same division into two residential (and class) areas by the railway as had occurred in Welwyn Garden City. That planning principles might be worth compromising for a gain of goodwill did not seem to occur to many planners. The Corporation favourably received Council suggestions for the creation of an artificial lake and lorry parks; it had taken scrupulous care to preserve the cricket ground, the avenue of lime and horse chestnut trees and had not dared shave a foot off any of Stevenage's six Roman barrows. The Ministry had scheduled 90 or so buildings as of special architectural or historic interest, but the 111 houses in Fairview Road suffered from being ordinary. A Corporation Official said in public that the houses in Fairview Road were not houses 'to perpetuate as monuments.' 'Of course they are not,' a resident retorted, 'who wants to live in a monument? They are, however, the homes of hundreds of decent and respectable, home-loving human beings.' The

Ministry now stated that 'the location of factories in the industrial area should be so arranged that the residential character of Fairview Road is preserved as long as possible ... The strength of the Development Corporation's case for acquiring Fairview Road properties ... can only be decided when they can prove that they are an essential part of the development of the whole industrial area.'

The Earl of Lytton, then seventy and president of the Garden Cities and Town Planning Association, told the inspector at the Ministry Inquiry of 1946 that 'it is carrying principle to the point of madness to insist that people who already live on [one] side of the railway and who are prepared to live there must vacate their houses and live on the other side, whether they like it or not.' But Ministry bureaucrats had fastened onto an ideal which they intended to realize. 'Present pain,' they maintained, 'was necessary to future achievement;' a doctrine easy to uphold, noted Orlans[10], if the sacrifice is not your own.

E M Forster, who had lived in Stevenage at one time and written *Howards End* there, voiced his feelings in a broadcast for the BBC, subsequently published in *The Listener* on 11 April 1946.

'I was brought up as a boy in one of the home counties in a district which I still think the loveliest in England. There is nothing special about it: it is agricultural land and could not be described in terms of beauty spots. It must always have looked much the same. I have kept in touch with it, going back to it as to an abiding city and still visiting the house which was my home [Rooks' Nest], for it is occupied by old friends. A farmer is through the hedge and when the farmer there was eight years old and I was nine we used to jump up and down on his grandfather's straw ricks and spoil them. Today he is a grandfather himself ... Life went on there as usual until this spring. Then someone who was applying for a permit to lay a waterpipe was casually informed that it would not be granted since the whole area had been commandeered. Commandeered for what? Hadn't the war ended? Appropriate officials now arrived from London and announced that a satellite town for sixty thousand people is to be built there. The people now living and working there are doomed; it is death for them and they move in a nightmare ... Anyhow the satellite town has pushed them off as completely as it will obliterate the ancient and delicate scenery. Meteorite town would be the better name, for it has fallen on them out of a blue sky.'

'Well,' says the voice of planning and progress, 'why this sentimentality? People must have houses.' 'They must, and I think of working class friends in London who have to bring up four children in two rooms, and many are even worse off. But I cannot equate the problem. It is a collision of loyalties. I cannot free myself from the conviction that something irreplaceable has been destroyed, and that a little piece of England has died as surely as if a bomb had hit it.'

In contrast, Orlans concluded there were many people indifferent to the New Town proposals. Planning Politics and the 'Brave New World' interested only a limited portion of the population; the rest were more preoccupied with dogs, beer, gardening or their digestion, especially if their property or livelihood was unlikely to be affected. The crucial fight on the New Town was fought not in local assemblies, ballot boxes and streets, but in judicial and Ministerial chambers where law and learned argument reigned supreme. Whatever may have been the nation's verdict in the General Election of 1945 which swept Labour to power, it was not a verdict on the Greater London Plan. The politics which determined the fate of Stevenage had an intricate history of their own, formulated by professional politicians, civil servants and planners according to their terms of reference. The will of the electorate could scarcely have been consulted on this issue, important as it was to many Londoners and the people of Stevenage.

Hence, a state of apathy quickly emerged, with townspeople remarking: 'People don't seem to have any choice about it.' 'We were not consulted. We were never consulted. It is nothing to do with us. What we do or think makes no difference. Why bother?' Ignorance helped generate apathy. Patient scrutiny of the maps of the New Town, the models, the posters and the diagrams was required before much could be learned from them. One viewer commented: 'I don't know anything about town and country planning. Anyway they'll do it wrong.' Excessive debate and minimal action also resulted in apathy. The more than three years in which planners did nothing but plan made supporters and opponents alike lose heart.

In the end Fairview Road survived more or less intact, not obviously a carbuncle on an otherwise pristine architectural scheme. Although the road carries more traffic, the houses have mostly been improved. The house at 98 now sits in front of an Infants' School. The angry voices and the sound of farm carts alike have drifted away.

Fig 23 – The old Parish church of St Nicholas, around 1920, from the east end. Drawing from a photograph in Stevenage in Old Photographs[12] *(courtesy Stevenage Museum).*

6

The Culpins – A Family History

The Name Culpin

Grandpa Culpin would sit at the large table in the front room at 5 Basils Road laying out his cards for patience. From time to time, he would place one finger against his nostril and sniff rather loudly, the consequence of the respiratory infirmity which may run in the family along with the noses. A heavy, dark table cloth was the constant companion of the dining room table which was only pushed back at tea time. My grandfather was Herbert Miall Culpin, kind and benevolent towards his grandchildren and always ready to show us his summerhouse full of bee-keeping equipment. I will return to him in the next chapter.

Although the Culpins were well known in Stevenage, the name was unusual. There were no other Culpins in the locality except for our relatives. The name appears in England from the late 16th century. For instance, the marriage of Thomas Culpin to Joan Goodlud is recorded for 30 October 1575 in the parish of Tinwell in Rutland and in Seaton, Rutland, Christopher Culpin married Isabel Field in 1579. Neither is on the direct family line. The majority of the citings come from Bedfordshire, Northamptonshire, Lincolnshire and Rutland, although Marriage Registers show Culpins marrying in Yorkshire from 1603, in London from 1673, in Leicestershire from 1793, Hampshire from 1685, Cambridgeshire from 1766 and Lancashire from 1808. Most of the families were involved in agriculture. The Yorkshire and Lancashire records might conceivably be misspellings of the more common Culpan/Culpen, which was relatively prevalent in the north of England. Some Culpins emigrated to Australia, New Zealand, to the United States and possibly to Canada.

The origin of the Culpin name is obscure. A possible Huguenot link or a connection with Scotland has been suggested by various members of the family. Verula Rogers seems certain of the Huguenot link. I am indebted to them for much of the following and especially the reminiscences about family members long dead. In particular I should mention Verula Rogers née Culpin and her brother, Francis de Montford Culpin, and also Frances Jo and Stephen MacKeith. Frances' father was Dr Millais Culpin, well known in the field of Industrial Psychology and Professor at the London School of Hygiene and Tropical Medicine.

If I were a Blackbird ...

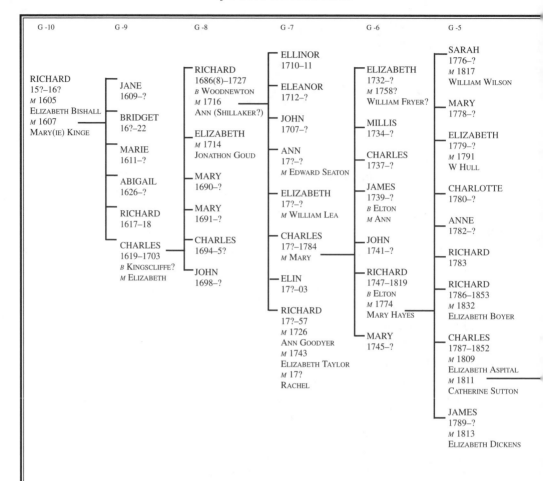

| G -10 | G -9 | G -8 | G -7 | G -6 | G -5 |

Fig 24 – Culpin Family Tree showing 10 generations back to the early Seventeenth Century. The connection with the first Richard and his son Charles needs to be confirmed. Details off this direct line have been omitted for clarity

Generally, I have tried to identify the relation of the person described to Herbert Miall Culpin. The generations are enumerated according to the schema: Generation 0 for my generation, with negative numbers to denote earlier generations. A Family Tree traces the Culpins back 10 generations to Richard and Charles Culpin of Northamptonshire.

THE CULBIN SANDS

Clifford Culpin, Herbert's nephew, told me in a letter that his father Ewart was a great romantic and claimed that the Culbin Sands on the Moray Firth, to the west of the river Findhorn, were the origin of the name

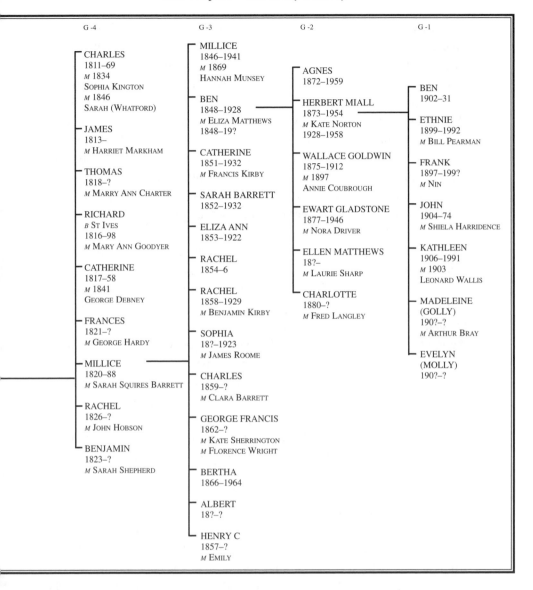

G -4	G -3	G -2	G -1

Culpin. Ewart maintained that the sands, where a submerged village is said sometimes to appear with fruit trees in full blossom, were Culpin estates. Clifford's brother Howard reminded me that despite a Highland trait of pronouncing 'b' as 'p', the Gaelic Culbin was pronounced Coubine, not Culpin; and from 1460 the barony of Culbin was in the possession of the Kinnairds. There is no trace of the name Culpin in a number of source books on Scottish surnames according to the English Surnames Project at the University of Leicester, neither does it appear amongst the usual sources of English surnames.

The word 'culpon' is derived from the old French 'colpon' and means ' a piece cut off, a portion, a strip, or as a verb to cut up, to ornament with strips of different coloured material'. Howard believes that the Culpins were of Huguenot origin and came from North West France, fleeing the country just before the St Bartholomew's Day Massacre of 1572, when Protestants were murdered by Catholics. Possibly they found refuge in Vienna and then moved, as weavers, to Lincolnshire. Many became farmers. Two are listed in the *Civil Service Year Book* as experts – one on farming machinery – and the number of Culpins in the Lincolnshire telephone directory runs into double figures. Frances Bygrave (nee Pearman) – my mother was her great aunt – thought it possible the Culpin name was Dutch in origin.

All Culpins, according to Frances MacKeith, are gentle people with a strand of deathly obstinacy in their make up. Usually, they have been non-conformists. A forebear from Downham Market in Norfolk spent time in Norwich gaol for non-payment of church tythes. Millice (G –4), both a Dissenter and an articulate debater, used to have lively discussions with the Rector of Stevenage, the Revd Jowitt. Millice was keen on education and ran classes for his employees once the working day was over, schooling them in the three Rs. Bertha Culpin maintained that Church of England folk thought it heresy to raise men beyond the condition to which God had called them. The Revd Jowitt had a large family and, at a stage at which eight daughters had been produced, his wife ascended the pulpit to announce: 'My dear friends, you will be pleased to know that God has blessed us with a son'[17].

CULPINS IN NORTHANTS

The first Culpins I have been able to trace lived in Northamptonshire. This branch of the family moved into the village of Woodnewton, Northants, from nearby Kings Cliffe around the mid-1600s. The family appear throughout the late 1600s in the court rolls of the manor of Woodnewton and quite soon seem to have become prominent in the village. They are listed as 'homagin juror' (someone who holds lands by homage or fealty, *eg* a manorial tenant). Charles Culpin (G -9) does not appear in the Baptismal or Burial registers for Woodnewton, but evidence from the court rolls supports his presence in this village from around 1640. He may be the Charles Culpin whose baptism is recorded in the Kings Cliffe Register for 1619. Charles Culpin of Woodnewton was a copyholder of land and property between at least 1665–1703, a churchwarden and someone who sat on the local court.

Charles was possibly the son of Richard Culpin (G -10?) who married Elizabeth Bishall in Kings Cliffe in 1605; she died the same year without having children. In 1607 Richard married Mary (or Marie) Kinge. She bore him four daughters, Bridget (d. 1622), Jane (*b* 1609), Marie (*b* 1611) Abigail (*b* 1626), and two sons, Richard (*b* 1617) who lived for a year, and Charles, baptised in 1619 (G-9?).

CHARLES (G -9) AND RICHARD (G -8)

Charles Culpin of Woodnewton (1619–1703) had a wife called Elizabeth and she appears to have borne six children, Richard around 1686 to 1688 (G -8), Elizabeth 1689, Mary 1690, Mary 1691, Charles 1694 and John 1698, all baptised in Woodnewton.

Richard (G -8, 1686?–1728), the eldest son, was a tailor and Copyholder (a person who held land by Copyhold Tenure, *ie* by copy of the Manorial Court Roll). He married Ann, who bore him three sons (Richard, Charles, John) and five daughters (Ann, Elizabeth, Ellinor, Eleanor, Elin). Ann was buried in Woodnewton in 1724. Richard in his will, 'being sick but perfect in memory and remembrance, praise be to God' left his son Charles (G -7) Five pounds, his son John Five pounds, his grandson Edward Seaton Five pounds and his son Richard Trustee for the same. His daughter Elizabeth was left Five pounds, a bed and bedding, 5 pewter dishes, 3 plates, 2 kettles – the best and the worse one. All the rest of his lands, houses, leases, tenements and goods was left to his son Richard. The will was witnessed by Jonathon Goud and Mark Desborough and signed by Richard Culpin, RC, his mark.

CHARLES (G -7) AND RICHARD (G -6, 1747–1819)

The line through Charles (G -7) runs onto my own great-great-grandfather Millice Culpin.

A Culpin branch through Richard (and Ann Goodyear or Goodyer), Richard (m. Elizabeth Wade) and then Richard (1766-1828, m. Sarah Burbidge) moved to Castor near Peterborough in Northamptonshire. The history of this branch, many of whose descendants worked on the railways, is available on the Internet[18]. In the late 1700s the family hit hard times and had to sell their land and buildings. After Richard died the children moved to other villages (to find work), leaving their mother alone in the village. She may have died a few years later as a pauper.

Charles (G -7) himself was buried from the workhouse in 1784. Charles had married Mary (?), who is buried in Elton, Huntingdonshire. They had seven children: Elizabeth (*b* 1732), Millis (*b* 1734), Charles (*b* 1737), James (*b* 1739), John (*b* 1741), Mary (*b* 1745) and Richard (G –6, *b* 1747).

Richard (G-6), Charles' son, married Mary Hayes in 1774 in Elton, Hunts, and the family line runs through him and his son, Charles (G-5).

Richard and Mary Hayes *(b* 1750) had nine children, five of whom were girls (Sarah, *b* 1776, Mary *b* 1778, Elizabeth *b* 1779, Charlotte *b* 1780, Anne *b* 1782, Richard *b* 1783, d. 1 month, Richard *b* 1786, Charles (G-5) *b* 1787 and James *b* 1789.

CHARLES CULPIN (G -5, 1787–1852,) AND HIS CHILDREN

Charles born in 1787, probably at or near St Ives, Huntingdon, married Catherine Watts in 1811. She was related to Isaac Watts, the writer of 'When I survey the wondrous cross' and was a widow whose married name was Sutton. She had a son, John, by her first marriage who became a Veterinary Surgeon and practised at Sawtry, between St Ives and Peterborough. Charles Culpin lived in St Ives on the site of Oliver Cromwell's gateway and was an Agricultural Instrument Merchant. He may be the Charles Culpin recorded in a St Ives 1839 Directory as living in Wisbech Road, although this Culpin is reported to be a blacksmith. The Pigot & Co Commercial Directory for 1823–4 records a William Culpin of St Ives trading as blacksmith. Whether he was a relative is unknown.

Charles' eldest son, and eldest of nine children, was also called Charles. He was born in 1812 or 1811 and took on the Agricultural Instrument business. Charles' eight brothers and sisters were Richard born 1816, Catherine born 1817, Thomas born in 1818, Frances born 1821 who married George Hardy, my great-great-grandfather Millice Culpin (G -4) born in 1820, Rachel born 1826, Ben born 1823 and James born 1813 – 'The Apostle of the Sol-fa' (see Stevenage Methodists). Millice is a family name with the Culpins and a variant on Miles or Millais. The Parish Register for St Mary's, Marylebone, records a Millis Culpin marrying Alice Usher in 1789, possibly a nephew of Richard Culpin (G -6).

A little information on this generation has come from Verula Rogers and Frances MacKeith. Thomas Culpin, brother of Millice, born 1818 and married to Mary Ann Charter, was an engineer who learned to ride a penny-farthing bicycle when he was over eighty. Richard Culpin born in 1816 had two daughters, Harriet and Carrie, and was in the boot business. Thomas' brother Charles had at least two sons, Millice and Roebuck O'Connell. The strangely named Roebuck O'Connell seems to have predeceased his father.

Rachel, sister of Millice, became Rachel Hobson and had two sons, Eustace and Charles. Ben, brother of Millice, born in 1823, became a Congregational Minister; he had at least three children, two daughters, Lizzie and Sarah, and a son James. Catherine, sister of Millice, was a dressmaker who married George Debney in 1841. In 1852 George and two children, followed two years later by Catherine with four remaining children, sailed to Port Phillip in the New Hebrides.

The Culpins – A Family History

The 1881 British Census has Millice Culpin, aged 61, head of a family of five, living in Albert Street, Stevenage. His place of birth is recorded as St Ives, Huntingdon, his occupation – Currier, Legging and Upper Manufacturer, employing 4 men, 1 boy and 5 women. In Kelly's Directory for 1867 he is listed as an insurance agent for Manchester Fire and in Kelly's Directory for 1882 as 'Culpin, Millice and sons – Curriers, upping and legging manufacturers.' The eldest son in the house was Charles, who was then 21 and working as a leather cutter (currier), presumably for his father.

MILLICE CULPIN (G -4, 1820–1888) AND SARAH SQUIRES BARRETT (1823–1915)

Verula Rogers recalls that her grandparents, Millice and Sarah Squires, were the first to marry in the Free Church in Buntingford, near Walkern. Sarah Squires Barrett was born in 1823 at Downham, Cambridgeshire, the daughter of Joseph Barrett and Anne Crossley. Anne was supposedly the daughter of Sir Francis Crossley later to become Baron Somerleyton of Somerleyton Hall in Suffolk, a Halifax carpet magnate and great benefactor to that city. He, we can assume, was not best pleased to discover that his daughter Anne had eloped with his steward, Joseph Barrett. Anne was reportedly disowned, but Verula Rogers believes there was a later reconciliation. Sarah Squires used to talk to her daughters about visits to a large country house. Joseph and Anne had at least four

Fig 25 – Five of Ben Culpin's sisters and his brother George Francis, probably taken about 1928. Front row, left to right: Sarah Barrett Culpin, Catherine Kirby (Culpin), Sophia Roome (Culpin); back row, left to right: Rachel Culpin, George Francis, Bertha Culpin.

children, Sarah, William, Ephraim and Anne. They were to re-unite with the Culpin family in a later generation, for William's daughter Clara married Charles Culpin, second son of Millice and Sarah Squires. They were cousins. Anne (daughter of Joseph) became a Mrs H Hill and her daughter on marriage became a Flinders. The descendants of this branch of the family live in Queensland. Millice and Sarah Culpin are buried in the family grave at St Nicholas' Church, Stevenage.

THE CHILDREN OF MILLICE AND SARAH SQUIRES CULPIN

Millice and Sarah had thirteen children. By 1881, Ben Ephraim Lamartine (BEL) Culpin (born 1848, my great-grandfather, G -3) had left home. He was 32 and already the head of a household, a Boot Dealer and Assistant Overseer, living in Stevenage High Street. Catherine had been born in 1851 and Rachel in 1858. Rachel was named after a sister who died within two or three years of birth; after marriage she became Rachel Kirby. At the Census of 1881 Sophia had left the household to marry James Roome. Rachel Kirby sent my Auntie Ethnie the photograph of six of Millice's children dated 1928. By then George Francis would have been about 66. He and his sisters comfortably confront the camera with visages ranging from the severe to the serene. Bertha benignly holds a large tabby cat and looks like my mother. This photograph was passed by Ethnie to her grandaughter, Frances Bygrave.

CATHERINE (KATE), RACHEL AND SARAH CULPIN (G -3)

Kate and Rachel lived to a good age and both married Kirbys. Kate married Francis Joshua Kirby who was a Baptist Minister in Ramsgate; he wrote the music hall song: *The boy I know is up in the gallery* according to Verula Rogers. However, the Census of 1881 records Catherine Kirby aged 30 living in Hellards Road, Stevenage, the wife of a builder. Living with her was her sister, Rachel, aged 23, occupation: machinist. Verula Rogers remembers her Aunt Kate as a sweet lady, her knickname was 'kissie'. Although Kate bore no children of her own, she and Francis adopted a little girl. Rachel was later to marry Francis' brother, Benjamin Kirby, but she was widowed after two or three months. Rachel and Kate are in the 1928 photograph, taken about a year before Kate died.

Sarah trained as a nurse in London and became the matron of a hospital (Warneford?) in Edinburgh. Before achieving this, she had acted as a nurse to doctors in private practice whose clients included Mrs Pullar (of Perth) and Lady Minto, Vicerene of India. She was given an exquisite ivory broach by Lady Minto. She was asked to nurse at Balmoral but chose to return to Stevenage to nurse her mother. Sarah never married and attended the Wesleyan Church in Stevenage (see Stevenage Methodists), at one stage living in Weston Road Stevenage with her sister Bertha, just two doors away from Auntie Ethnie.

GEORGE FRANCIS CULPIN (G -3)

George went to Alleyne's Grammar School in Stevenage. He was ambitious and competed with his cousin George Hardy, the son of the George Hardy who had married Frances Culpin and was 'Uncle George'. Uncle George ran a school or college – perhaps Rothbury School or College, Stroud Green – for young gentlemen who were dissenters and barred from attending other schools at that time. Cousin George became an actuary, later chairing the Finance Committee for Lloyd George's National Insurance Scheme and subsequently being knighted.

George Francis Culpin joined the War Office, ending in the Lands Branch for which he was chief examiner to the Directorate of Lands. In the 1881 Census he was nineteen and working as a clerk in the lower division of the War Office. During the Great War he worked for Sir Howard Frank of Knight, Frank & Rutley. Verula Rogers remembers him (her father) taking her to Caxton Hall, where his part of the War Ofice operated and showing her his spacious room. He was awarded the OBE in 1919 for services rendered during the war. The family lived in St Albans (Verulam) and this seems to have been the basis of Verula's christian name. Later they moved to a farm in Essex as George Francis liked the country life. He was driven by his groom, Beckingsale, to the railway station six miles away. Some years earlier, George Francis seems to have left – and presumably divorced – his first wife, Kate Sherrington, with her five daughters (Mabel, Norah, Gwendoline and twins, Daisie and Maggie) and married Florence Sarah Wright of Stevenage. 'Bad Uncle George' as Auntie Ethnie called him! By Florence, George Francis had daughters Annabell and Ivy, who died in infancy, and Verula Mary (Rogers) and a son, Francis de Montford (Uncle Monty) Culpin. Both George Francis and his son Monty had a strong interest in Culpin family history.

CHARLES CULPIN (G -3)

Charles was born in 1859. At the census of 1881 he still lived with his father Millice in Albert Street, Stevenage, and working as leather cutter. Subsequently he was Registrar of Marriages for Stevenage, with his brother George Francis as deputy. Like George Francis he seems to have been one of the darker sheep of the family. He first married his cousin, Clara Barrett, by whom he had four children, Elsie Bertha Barrett, Millice Charles Lalouche, Mabel (?) and Mildred (?). He then, according to Verula, ran off with his children's governess and sailed to America. She believes there was a bigamous marriage to Gertrude and a warrant prepared for his arrest, which may have prompted a change of name to Carey-Culpin. Charles and Gertrude had two sons, Walter and Frank. Walter Carey-Culpin, a Lieutenant-Colonel in the US Army, visited the UK during the Second World War. Charles also returned to England briefly and Verula's mother found him charming. This was I suppose after Clara had died. Either Frank or Walter was a civil engineer working, at one time, on measures to control Mississippi floods. The other brother became an Agricultural Advisor to the Mexican Government.

BERTHA, ELIZA ANN AND SOPHIA CULPIN (G -3)

Bertha lived from 1866 until 1965, unmarried but much loved, a 'grand person' according to Frances MacKeith and a fount of information about the family. She would describe how her father took her to Knebworth House to hear Charles Dickens give one of his readings. Dickens was a friend of Lord Lytton, the owner of Knebworth House, and seems to have made regular visits there and also to Stevenage. *Bleak House* is supposed to have been written in Stevenage. The old pub *Our Mutual Friend* on the Great North Road in Stevenage is associated with him and Dickens provides an impression of Stevenage High Street in 1861 in *Tom Tiddler's Ground*[19].

'The village street was like most other village streets: wide for its height, silent for its size, and drowsy in the dullest degree. The quietist little dwellings with the largest of window-shutters (to shut up Nothing as carefully as if it were the Mint, or Bank of England), ... a score of weak little plath-and-plaster cabins hung in confusion about the Attorney's red-brick house ... Some of the small tradesman's houses, such as the crockery-shop and the harness makers, had a Cyclops window in the middle gable, within an inch or two of its apex, suggesting that some forlorn rural Prentice must wriggle himself into the apartment horizontally when he retired to rest, after the manner of the worm. So bountiful in its abundance was the surrounding country, and so lean and scant the village, that one might have thought the village had sown and planted everything it once possessed, to convert the same into crops.'

Bertha would have been unlikely to have gone anywhere near a public house and she visited the theatre only once during her lifetime, accompanying her nephew Millais Culpin. The youngest daughter of a large family, Bertha was not much older than Millais. Bertha worked for the GPO for 36 years; later she helped at, and then took over, the Fraser drapery business in Albert Street, Stevenage. Thomas Fraser was her brother-in-law. For a time she lived in Weston Road, two doors down from my Auntie Ethnie with her sisters Rachel and Sarah.

Eliza Ann Culpin, who died about 1922, married Thomas Robert

Fraser who ran the draper's shop in Albert Street. She attended the Strict Baptist Church in Albert Street (now demolished). My mother remembers attending services with them, Aunt Eliza usually well-supplied with sweets to 'keep children quiet' during long sermons. Uncle Tom, my mother said, was a big, jolly man and Aunt Eliza a kindly, motherly soul.

Sophia Culpin (Verula's Aunt Sophie) married James Roome. They ran a large store in Upminster, Essex.

BEN EPHRAIM LAMARTINE (1848–1928, G -3) AND ELIZA MATTHEWS (1848–19?)

Ben or BEL Culpin was closely associated with the Methodist Church in Stevenage (see Stevenage Methodists). He was born in 1848 in Buntingford, Hertfordshire. The 1881 census finds him, age 32, the head of the household living with his wife and four children and dealing in boots. He is listed as Assistant Overseer. Presumably his father Millice still ran the business. They lived in Stevenage High Street at that time, although later they moved to 7 Basils Road to the house next door to his son, Herbert Miall Culpin. The signature of the enumerator on the declaration of the Census Return for 1881 is that of BEL Culpin. The family photograph of BEL with a General Smuts' beard is undated and signed Sarah (or Dora) Head. Ben's business seems to have been located in Albert Street. Clearly Ben was a non-conformist or Dissenter but of what exact persuasion is unclear. Despite his close links with the Stevenage Methodist Church, he was to found the Bunyan Baptist Church in Stevenage on the plot of land just next door to his house. A plaque records the debt the church owes to him, although the engraved foundation stone which I remember seeing as a boy has now disappeared from sight behind a newly added porch. Frances Bygrave suggests he may also have attended the Strict Baptist Chapel in Albert Street.

Ben married Eliza Matthews whose portrait confirms my mother's description of her: 'A small little lady with bright blue eyes and white hair, and full of fun.' My mother used to go round to her grandmothers and help make the beds and so on. Eliza told her she disliked needlework at school and, one day, dropped her needle during a sewing class. Getting down on her hands and knees she proceeded to look for it with her eyes closed so that a return to sewing might be delayed. Of course, some tell-tale-tit had to call out: 'Please Miss, Eliza Matthews is looking for her needle with her eyes shut'. Reprimanded, Eliza's response was that she was hoping the needle would shine in the dark.

Ben and Eliza had six children: Agnes born in 1872, Herbert Miall in 1973, Wallace F (Walter) in 1875, Ewart Gladstone in 1877, Ellen Matthews (Nellie) in 18?? and Charlotte in 1880. Ben and Eliza left

Fig 26a – Sara Head's portrait of Ben Ephraim Lamartine Culpin

Fig 26b – Sara Head's portrait of Eliza Matthews.

Fig 27 – Charlotte and Ellen Culpin, daughters of BEL Culpin, photographed around 1890 in a Hitchin photographic studio.

Stevenage when their grandchildren were still fairly young. They moved first to Romford, then to Crayford and finally to Battle in Sussex. My mother remembers visiting them in Battle in 1923.

MILLICE CULPIN (G -3)

Before dealing more fully with Ben and Eliza's children, I would like to say more about Millice Culpin, the younger brother of Ben, and his side of the family. Frances MacKeith, his grandaughter, recalls that he became a stern rationalist. Much of what follows is from *An Autobiography* by his son Millais[20]. Millice was a doctor in general practice in Stoke Newington. He lived in a Georgian house facing a main road along which waggons loaded with farm produce rumbled on their way to town in the mornings, returning later bearing the dung from the stables of London. Millice married Hannah Munsey and they had probably eleven children, including Ernest, Dorothy, Rose, Millais and Clarence. Clarence was killed in the First World War. The Commonwealth War Commission records the death of C H Culpin, Australian Infantry, A I F, for 16 April 1918. Ernest, who was an army doctor in the First World War, had one son Keith who was an architect.

The yellow fogs of London made Millice ever more chesty with each winter. He eventually sold his practice and took the family to Queensland, setting up a new practice in Brisbane. Frances MacKeith visited Brisbane in 1940 and remembers seeing a 'Culpin Hall'. In a letter to Frances, Millice mentions that his infant sister, Rachel, was denied burial in the churchyard at Stevenage. Millice seems to have corresponded with Reginald Hine, who recounts in Hitchin Worthies[6] that Millice Culpin told him of going with his father in 1859 to visit the Hermit of Redcoats Green. The hermit, even though he disliked Dissenters, was so fond of children that he gave them a half-crown for the Wesleyan Sunday School and a half-crown for the Baptist Sunday School.

Millice's son, Millais, had a career of great distinction and is well enough known in the field of Psychology to deserve a potted biography of his own.

MILLAIS CULPIN (G -2)

Millais was born in 1874, the name having no artistic connection but a variant on the family name Millice. He went to the local school for seven years, whose head, he says, had a single educational plan – Give them stuff to learn from a book and up to six handers if they don't know it. Lick your thumb between strokes. The experience made Millais a 'doubter of authority, slow to recognise when it was on my side and even then

Fig 28 – Millais Culpin

diffident and mistrustful.' At fifteen, he continued his education at the Grocers' Company School where he obtained a scholarship and became an enthusiastic entomologist. He used his scholarship money to make one of many trips to Wicken Fen, near Ely, a heaven for bug hunters.

After his father had moved the family to Australia, he tried many ways of earning a living. He spent three months at a gold rush where an illiterate but skilled miner taught him how to use a shovel and work a damper. He took a job as a schoolmaster at Laura, a township on Cape York Peninsula about 15° south of the equator. To meet the educational needs of a shifting population, and providing people would put up a structure that would keep out the weather, the Government agreed to pay the salary of a suitable master, *ie* someone who could read and write and do a bit of figuring. There were Aborigines all round, but it did not occur to anyone that their children should also be allowed to attend the school. On promotion to a bigger school, he disliked the change. He decided to quit teaching and use his savings to follow an old ambition to study medicine. He knew he would be hard up but managed to win an entrance scholarship to the London Hospital. A number of his letters home from his post at Laura have survived.

He seems to have relished the intellectual challenge of much of his teaching, but found himself puzzled and ill at ease with lectures which adumbrated an explanation through speculative theory. He cites as an example a lecture he heard on Ehrlich's side-chain theory of immunity. He had, he says, an uneasy, almost obsessional, urge to satisfy himself. Furthermore 'this was the dark age of psychology' and various cases, pronounced upon by some consultant, left him feeling there was something more to it he ought to know. There was general unease, as shown by the common lament that, with the advance of scientific medicine, the old-style practitioner who 'knew his patient's constitution' was disappearing.

Millais found surgery, perhaps because of its relative objectivity, more satisfying than medicine. He qualified in 1902 (MRCS, LRCP) and returned to Queensland. However, by 1904 he was back in England doing house appointments at the London (MB, BS, 1905, London). He served as both an ophthalmic as well as a general house surgeon and took his FRCS in 1907. A contact at the hospital enabled him to obtain a partnership in Shanghai and see the Old China before the revolution of 1911. His partner was reportedly killed during the Boxer Riots. Shanghai was described as a 'nervy place', but for the foreigner was luxurious and artificial. Millais, reflecting on his time there, later recognised various psychogenic conditions which he had failed to understand at the time. In his paper, *An Examination of Tropical Neurasthenia*[21] he contrasts the psychological effects of life in China with life in Queensland where so-called neurasthenia was scarcely known.

In 1913 he married Ethel Maude Bennett, deciding to return home and set up practice in the South of England. After the wedding the couple travelled by Manila and Timor to Australia to visit his old pupils in Laura. War broke out in 1914 as they were on their way back to England. Coming up the Channel they heard the distant thunder of the Battle of the Marne. At The London, he was given a war-time job as surgical registrar, but in November became a temporary lieutenant in the RAMC and was made surgical member of a Board for officers in London.

WAR NEUROSES

At that time the existence of war neuroses was unsuspected. Officers appearing before the Board with obvious hysterical conditions and less definable ones soon to be known as shell-shock were, scarcely without exception, receiving diagnoses of some physical condition. He cites a couple of examples – one man had a condition labelled tubercular disease of the tarsus but really a hysterical clubfoot and a similar case was diagnosed 'talipes varus following osteo-arthritis'. In reality, each man had inverted his foot by muscular action and walked on its outer edge as if he had a kind of club-foot. Hysteria enabled him to maintain the deformity, and some swelling followed because of the immobility in a dependent position. Men had spent months in hospital with their fictitious diseases waiting to be invalided out. But the false diagnosis was the easier way out, both for the Board and for the patient. Millais was assured that the War Office would not accept a diagnosis of hysteria. He prepared notes about hysteria and a copy was sent to the M Os of neighbouring units. Many problem cases arrived for Millais to see. His technique was to take the man into a side room where, after an initial 'This is man to man', Millais told him his opinion as a surgeon and invited a reply. Often he was roundly abused and sworn at, but an unexpected number thanked him, declaring it was the first time anyone had taken much interest in them. Occasionally, one broke down and with emotion told his hard-luck story. Millais learned, among other things, that a man might have an hysterical symptom and still be a decent and reasonable citizen. Millais was required to inspect neighbouring auxiliary hospitals and convalescent homes, where a quick run around confirmed that the condition was widespread. At the time, attempts to explain shell-shock invoked notions of the after-effects of concussion, separated synapses, dissociated cerebral centres and punctiform haemorrhages. Millais came to see such explanations as fantasy unsupported by any proper evidence. He states that he 'had not learnt how to spell psychology, but could see that here was something the man himself was doing'.

Returning from Paschendaele and the Somme, he sought to discuss his views with a few officers in high places. He told Sir John Collie, then powerful in the world of pensions, that a third of his pensioners were wrongly diagnosed as suffering from organic disease. Sir John's reply was: 'Yes, that's rather an underestimate. But if you try to press this point you will make yourself very unpopular.' Colonel Aldren Turner, a neurologist, altered his career, telling him that the Army had more surgeons than it needed but could not get people to help with cases of hysteria and the like. Millais was sent on a training course to Maghull where he benefited from the teaching of Captain Bernard Hart, Professor Pear and Major Rows. Later, Millais was transferred to Ewell Military Hospital and began to give lectures at the London Hospital on war psychoneuroses. He was demobilized in 1919 and gained his M.D. at London University with a thesis entitled: *Psychoneuroses of War and Peace.* In 1949, he felt that this work, although narrow in its outlook compared with more modern writing, described methods and results of abreaction that would stand comparison with anything achieved today by the use of drugs. An appointment as a lecturer on the psychoneuroses at the London Hospital was offered to him and he settled down as a psychotherapist. Around this time, he underwent an instructional analysis and 'learned what it felt like to experience the emotion of belief (relief?) when my own unconscious material came to the surface.'

MILLAIS AND INDUSTRIAL PSYCHOLOGY

In the twenties, Millais entered the field of industrial psychology. May Smith and Eric Farmer had been appointed by the Industrial Health Research Board to investigate telegraphists' cramp. Initially regarded as a fatigue phenomenon, they came to suspect a strong psycho-pathological element. The Board brought in Millais Culpin to investigate further. He examined many subjects with cramp who turned out to be suffering from severe psychoneuroses upon which the cramp developed in response to the external situation[22].

He compared a group of telegraphists already diagnosed as having cramp with a similar group telegraphically efficient. Among the former were many who had no disability except for certain letters. There were an unexpected number of psychoneurotic subjects among the non-cramp controls, rendering it likely that a similar incidence would be found in the general population. Millais and May Smith worked together for many years, investigating by personal interview the staff in Government departments, private firms, training schools and colleges, laundries, the

National Physical Laboratory, wherever they could get a foot in. May Smith shared the interviewing whilst carrying out the McDougall-Schuster dotting test, which statistically corroborated the results of the interview. They discovered much that is now common knowledge, although the discovery that about 30% of workers suffer from nervous symptoms which interfere with efficiency or happiness, and that symptoms in 6 – 8% are severe enough to send people to the consulting room of a specialist, took some time to soak in[23].

Millais was appointed to a part-time chair in Medical Industrial Psychology and a home found for him in the London School of Hygiene and Tropical Medicine. Students training for medical and industrial work in the fields of public health were taught about the psychological problems likely to be encountered. May Smith continued to work with him; industrial sickness next drew their attention and, as the war-time studies had found, they discovered that most psychoneurotic sickness was camouflaged as physical disease. Nystagmus, an oscillation of the eyeballs occurring in coal-miners in safety-lamp pits, was the next area of study. In 1930, the Miners' Nystagmus Committee of the Medical Research Council invited their assistance because the disorder was treated as an ocular disease within the sphere of the ophthalmologist and men disabled by it were legally entitled to compensation. However, the oscillation possibly arising because of bad illumination played a dubious part in the disability. Many men with well-marked oscillation continued to work and made no complaint. Others, claiming and receiving compensation, showed an oscillation only detectable by an expert. Moreover, all the disabling symptoms, except for a subjective movement of objects, were typically psychoneurotic. At the time, this was partially recognized, and said to be due to the nystagmus working through other channels unknown to the physiologist to produce a condition termed neurasthenia.

Smith and Culpin[24] found that, amongst 36 miners receiving compensation for nystagmus, only two showed notable oscillations and complained of movement of objects. 22 subjects showed no detectable oscillation, but 34 subjects were typically those who might be found at a clinic for psychoneurotic ex-servicemen or among the sufferers from telegraphists' cramp. Unlike telegraphists' cramp, the oscillation did not arise from the psychoneurosis but served as a peg upon which disability could be hung. Otherwise it had no relation to it either as cause or effect. Ophthalmologists had never studied the disabling symptoms. An ophthalmologist from a mining area, hearing Millais' opinion that a particular miner was disabled by severe phobias, replied that his compensation should be stopped and the man made to go down the pit again. The miners, with some excuse, regarded the denial of physical disease as an assertion that there was nothing the matter with them. Millais pleaded for the disabled miners to be provided with surface employment. He lost touch with the subject, but was horrified to read subsequent newspaper reports during the Second World War that Bevin Boys, who were psychologically unfit for underground work and tried to say so, were being sent to prison.

In 1920, Millais published a book on spiritualism, explaining that Janet's theory of dissociation provided him with insights into how honest people could believe they possessed occult powers, including that of water-divining. He comments that it was probably his nineteenth-century materialist up-bringing that made it impossible for him to accept evidence in favour of such things and for extra-sensory perception that satisfied some of his colleagues. However, having been convinced of the value of psychoanalysis, he could not understand why there was so much opposition to it. He thought that if a theory or general principle was clear to him it must be equally clear to others. But he was ready to be convinced that two apparent incompatibles might have to be accepted in the absence of adequate differentiating data and then he could tolerate the two. He said once that an uncle of his, a member of one of the more rigid religious sects (and maybe BEL Culpin), was perfectly convinced that his nephew was damned, but on this basis they got on excellently, and the latter bore him no ill will.

In 1944 he was elected President of the British Psychological Society. Millais retired in 1939 but continued to do some clinical work. To those in trouble he was the perfect physician, never grudging time or sympathy if he could help. Among his publications were: 'Practical Hints on Functional Disorders' *Brit Med J (1916)*; 'The Early Stages of Hysteria' *Brit Med J (1918)*; 'The Psychological Aspect of the Effort Syndrome' *Lancet (1920)* and 'Problem of the Neurasthenic Pensioner' *Br J Psych (1921)*.

Millais Culpin died on 14 September 1952, aged 78, as he lived, without fuss.

7

GRANDFATHER CULPIN AND HIS SIBLINGS

HERBERT MIALL CULPIN (1873–1954, G -2)

Grandpa Culpin's garden was full of enticements. Behind the beehives and a dense stand of blackcurrant bushes where you could crawl through luxuriant grass, lay the back of the Almshouses. Into their backyards, an ancient pensioner might suddenly emerge to empty a teapot or tend a flowerpot. At one end was the blankwalled rear of a tiny Municipal Baths, whose front was brass-handled and slightly mysterious, never apparently in use.

Fig 29 – Herbert Miall Culpin in a studio portrait by P Howard of Stevenage

Grandpa kept his beekeeping equipment in an old creosoted summer house, which once must have rotated. Inside on a hot summer's day your senses were assailed with the intense odours of beeswax and honey. Stacked haphazardly a smoke gun, spare hive frames and various boxes and crates cramped the space. Grandpa's long coat and hat with its attached fine netting hung from a hook on the wall. Equally tempting to meddlesome boys was his potting shed full of a jumble of tools and odds and ends all cobwebbed with disuse. At the furthermost reach of the garden was a door which led into a garage. In the gloom within, in a mystery of waxen glory, stood a prewar Standard Ten saloon car, a four door with worn leather seats. This was the fantasy chariot that would on

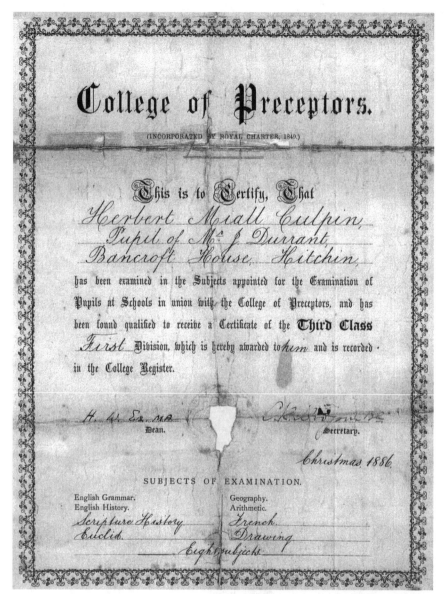

Fig 30 – Herbert Culpin's Certificate No. 11221 from the College of Preceptors for 1886

occasions take us all to the Suffolk or Norfolk coast, a vehicle which frazzled my mother's nerves after the War as she strove to tame its malign mechanics and which, after twenty miles, would induce in me without fail an attack of travel sickness. Grandpa was commendably patient when we had to stop on the roadside while I recovered.

Grandpa – Herbert Miall Culpin – was born in 1873. The Certificate from Christmas 1886 is from the College of Preceptors, recording the award of Third Class, First Division Passes in English Grammar, English History, Scripture, History, Euclid, Arithmetic, Geography, French and

Grandfather Culpin and his siblings

Fig 31 – The author's Grandparents, Herbert Miall and Kate, soon after their marriage, in a photograph by P Howard

Fig 32 – Mr and Mrs James Norton, great grandparents on Grandma Culpin's side of the family

If I were a Blackbird ...

Fig 33 – Grandma and Grandpa in old age in the garden of 5 Basils Road

Drawing. Herbert was then a pupil of Mr J Durrant of Bancroft House, Hitchin. He eventually worked for the Admiralty and became an Examiner of Accounts and looked after the victualling of ships. He was organist at the Bunyan Baptist Church just along the road from his house. Herbert married Kate Norton, the daughter of James Norton an engine driver. Kate had a sister Charlotte who married Frank Bird a bank clerk; Charlotte and Frank had four children. Kate also had a policeman brother, Tom. Kate's mother eventually went blind, and when she died Kate had to go and keep house for her father. What happened to her father when Kate married is not clear.

At Grandpa's wedding, the Best Man asked: "Why is Herbert more to me than he is to his wife?' – the answer 'Because he's my all (Miall) but he's only Her Bert!"

Herbert and Kate (1872–1958) stand in old age in front of the cherry tree that grew outside the kitchen window at 5 Basils Road *(Fig 33)*. My grandmother's stern expression is quite out of character, for her sense of humour matched that of Eliza Matthews.

She looks more like her usually benign self in a picture taken at a Church supper *(Fig 34)*. In later life, somewhat overweight, she had trouble with her legs. Varicose veins and ulcers, which would not heal, eventually confined her to bed in the front upstairs bedroom at 5 Basils Road. Her complaints seemed mysterious to us grandchildren. I imagined some strange degenerative process working its way in from her extremities, rather like frostbite, attacking first her toes, then her feet and her legs. Grandma's room was filled with rolls of bandages, lotions and doctor's surgery smells. She lay propped up with bolsters and cheerfully held court to visiting daughters and grandchildren. Herbert Miall had died some years before.

Fig 34 – Grandma at Church supper

The house in Basils Road retained some of its old features, especially at the back. The backdoor led into a scullery with a pantry to the side. Just to the right of the back door was a cast iron pump handle above a well, once the source of domestic water. The scullery had a brick boiler for washing clothes in one corner. Over the road from Number 5 stood the town fire station whose

If I were a Blackbird ...

Fig 35 – Stevenage Fire Station in Basils Road in 1937 with the old machines on display. Drawing from a photograph in Stevenage in Old Photographs[12]. *(With kind permission from Stevenage Museum)*

flashy antique machines wait in 1937 for the challenges of the Second World War.

Herbert and Kate had seven children: Frank, Ethnie, Ben, John, Kathleen, Madeleine (Golly) and Evelyn (Molly). Kathleen was my mother. I will return to them – all except Uncle Ben I knew quite well – after telling a little of the history of Herbert Miall's siblings.

AGNES, WALLACE, ELLEN AND CHARLOTTE CULPIN (G-2)

Agnes Culpin did not marry. Auntie Ethnie thinks this may have been because Agnes' mother hid the letters which had been sent to Agnes by her young man, perhaps because she did not want Agnes to leave home and be unable to look after her when she was old. Agnes, it seems, never knew her 'beau' had sent any letters and so she went with her parents to Battle. My mother remembers Aunt Aggie as a tall, rather stately lady with grey hair, quite fun to be with. She bred and sold canaries.

Wallace (Walter) Culpin ran a shoe shop in Stevenage. He and his wife, Ann, had a daughter Dorothy, but Walter died when Dorothy was only ten years old. Ann whose brother lived in Canada took Dorothy to live there with her brother.

Charlotte Ellard Culpin also emigrated to Canada with her husband, Fred Langley. They had a son called Graham. My mother's diaries mention Auntie Lottie visiting Stevenage in 1942.

Fig 36 – Uncle Laurie (Sharp) at Battle in 1927 with 'Dinah'

Ellen Culpin ran a private school over BEL Culpin's shop. She made items for soldiers during the Boer War helped by her sister Agnes. Both Auntie Ethnie and my Uncle Frank went to this school until they were eight. Ellen married a pork butcher called Laurie Sharp and eventually moved to Battle to live at Widdicombe Farm, only a few minutes' walk from her parents BEL and Eliza Culpin.

EWART GLADSTONE CULPIN (G -2)

Herbert Miall's other brother was Ewart. Ewart's sons, Clifford and Howard, have been the best source of information about him. Ewart, born in 1877, was an architect whose great expertise in the fields of housing and planning resulted in co-option to the London County Council. He was an Alderman, three times Vice-Chairman and then Chairman. As the first chairman of the LCC not to be knighted, Herbert Morrison told him: 'Ewart, Socialists don't accept titles !', unless, of course, you can become Lord Morrison of Lambeth.

At an obituary meeting of the LCC it was acknowledged that Ewart Culpin was more responsible than any man in Britain for bringing about the public acceptance (after 22 years of ardent campaigning and legislation) of the Green Belt policy.

The entry from *Who Was Who* 1941–1950 reads: 'Culpin, Ewart Gladstone. J P FRIBA. Officier de l'Ordre de la Couronne de la Belgique : Grand Officer of the Crown of Roumania : Commander of Order of the Black Star of Lenin : Trustee Official Czech Refugee Trust Fund. b. 3 Dec. 1877 s. of Ben Ephraim Lamartine and Eliza Culpin: m. 1903 Nora Driver. 2s. Educ. Alleyne's Grammar School Stevenage. Hitchin Grammar Sch. Secretary Garden City Association 1905. Founded International Garden Cities and Town Planning Association 1907: President Society Belge pour la Reconstruction de la Belgique : Chairman Standing Conference on London Regional Planning, 1926–46. Labour candidate North Islington 1924 ; Alderman LCC; Vice-Chm. LCC 1934–37; Chairman 1938–9; Pres. Incorporated Assoc. of Architects and Surveyors 1930 ; Pres TPI 1937–38; Publications: A number of booklets on Housing and Town Planning. Address: 18 Selwyn House, Manor Fields, Putney Hill S.W. 15. (Died 1 December 1946).

Verula Rogers was a cousin of Ewart. Because she was the youngest daughter of George Francis Culpin, most of her cousins were considerably older than her. When Ewart came to lecture on town planning to the Friends' School in Saffron Walden, her friends mistakenly told her they had been listening to her 'Uncle'.

CLIFFORD AND HOWARD CULPIN, SONS OF EWART (G -1)

Clifford was a successful architect and received an OBE for services to housing. He told me in a letter of 1978 of going to a Council School in (Saffron?) Walden, where he met his second cousin Verula. During the First World War he seems to have been half-starved and suffered from malnutrition, before going to West Ham Municipal College. Clifford became articled to his father's partner and attended evening classes for eight years before he qualified as an architect. He held junior posts in Local and Central Government Architects' Departments until, unexpectedly he says, he was taken into partnership with his father and was given the task of designing the Greenwich Civic Centre, now regarded as a landmark building.

After war service in India, he began specialising in housing, winning several open architectural competitions and four Housing Medals. He worked for the Queen in Windsor Park and designed the Croydon Airport re-development. He lectured on industrialised building in South Africa and New Zealand, on low-cost housing in Copenhagen, and prepared the Master Plan for the extension of Sheffield. Clifford became Vice-President of the Royal Institute of British Architects and was awarded an OBE. Clifford Culpin and Partners grew to employ over 100 staff spread over four offices. He retired in 1974 to have more time to paint and subsequently exhibited fairly widely. His wife, Mary, was a teacher of dancing and a choreographer. In 1978 she was still producing musical shows. Their daughter Jill died tragically while expecting her first child. She complained of stomach pains on stage and was told by her doctor it was just a bug, but she died four days later.

In the Culpin Liberal tradition, Clifford was active in local politics and was Constituency President for a number of years and after a Ward chairman.

In 1978 Howard Culpin had recently remarried after an unhappy first marriage; neither of his elder children was on speaking terms with him. Howard had been Features Editor of *Reynold's News,* but told his editor that the policy newly adopted would ruin the paper. Events apparently bore his prediction out. Howard was sacked on the spot. The NUJ got him about £4000 for wrongful dismissal. Fearing he would never get another job, Fleet Street being a young man's territory, in a matter of days he got a post with the Mail/Evening News Group. He worked for them until he was 65 and then part-time for the *Financial Times,* moving from the huge old Golding's Manor in Epping Forrest to live in the lodge. Howard was the author of at least two books: *The Newgate Noose* and *Underwater Exploration,* the latter published in four languages.

CHILDREN OF HERBERT CULPIN (G -1)

My Aunts and Uncles I knew well except for Uncle Ben who died in 1931. He was an engineer (born 1902) who worked on dust-cart design. Following a road accident, he lay in a coma in hospital for three months before he died.

If I were a Blackbird ...

Fig 37 – Ben Culpin in 1921 (age 17) photographed in the Cambridge Studio, 18 Mill Rd, Cambridge

FRANK AND JOHN

Frank was born in 1897 and was the eldest of seven children. Apprenticed at Phoenix Motors, Letchworth, he worked for Sir Frank Whittle, designer of the jet engine, before going to Cork to join the Ford Motor Company. He came back to Stevenage to marry 'Nin' Day, a neighbour of the family, transferring to Fords at Dagenham. Frank and Nin had one child, Michael, who became a lecturer at the University of Stirling. They moved to live near Exeter on Frank's retirement.

John Henry Culpin, born in 1904 and educated at Alleyne's Grammar School, became a bank manager for Barclay's Bank. With his nephews, Uncle John was a clown and a tease, entertaining us by pulling faces and

*Fig 38 – John Culpin in 1921
(aged 24) larking about*

making jokes. The photograph from the family album suggests his jokey sense of fun, which was rumoured to go down rather well with the ladies. Indeed he stayed a carefree bachelor for many years until he married a glamorous blonde in middle age. They both worked at the Hertford branch of Barclay's, Sheila Harridence a ledger clerk and John a Chief Clerk. Later, John Culpin became manager of the Baldock branch and he and his wife lived in a flat above the bank. After he retired, they moved to Long Bailey, North Road, Baldock. His ability to entertain the extended family was most in evidence at Christmas gatherings at 5 Basils Road. These would start in the afternoon, a big pile of presents heaped behind the sofa in the heavily curtained, back drawing room. Grandpa Culpin would hand these out before we all sat down to an elaborate high tea in the dining room. In the evening John would often show a home movie taken on holiday or of his wife and young family. They had two boys, Paul and John.

In 1963 John retired from the bank and began to devote much of his time to painting. In the nearly twelve years left to him, he had exhibitions at Stevenage, Norwich, Yarmouth and London. Before an exhibition at Hitchin Museum and Art Gallery, John in a brief interview said his first exhibition had been at Letchworth in 1962 and that this had been opened by Edward Swann, the founder of 'Painting Holidays'. John was asked to join the panel of artist tutors. Apart from attending two of these painting holidays, he never received any instruction in painting, claiming that art schools are more likely to be a handicap than a help. 'Most people who are sensitive to landscape can paint,' John said. 'A painting is only useful for the feeling it induces in other people.' His favourite medium was oils and his favourite subject landscapes. But, unless a subject 'sings' at him he will not paint it and, for this reason, rarely takes commissions. 'The quality of a painting is determined by your innermost thinking,' he said.

None of his pictures was highly priced because he disagreed strongly with the idea that, because a picture is expensive, it is better than one that

Fig 39 – John Culpin instructing a pupil on a painting course in 1971

is cheap. He made all his own frames and the pictures he sold helped him to buy more materials. One painting holiday participant wrote that, having instructed his pupils throughout the day, John gave up his evenings to discussion and criticism of their paintings. She found this fascinating and instructive; the comments were not too technical but very frank, and with the added incentive that a particularly good piece of work might be eligible for the annual exhibition in London.

Clifford Culpin, also a keen painter, only learnt of his cousin John's reputation when he himself went on a Galleon Painting holiday. John, he discovered, was one of their most popular tutors and loved by everyone. Clifford was taken aback to realise after John's death that they had lived so near each other, but never made contact. They had last met years back when both about 8 years old.

ARTISTIC GENES

Clearly the urge to paint is in the Culpin genes! But the Gods who give may also take away! My grandfather Herbert may have possessed a gene for colour blindness on his X-chromosome. Howard Culpin was asked by an Australian researcher to provide details of the sex-linked colour blindness running in the family. Howard sent the information and was relieved to find it ran only in BEL Culpin's branch.

This type of colour blindness, which I suffer from myself, is carried on the X-chromosome as a recessive characteristic. Females who have the corresponding dominant gene on their second X-chromosome do not express colour blindness, but act as carriers. They have a 50% chance of passing the recessive gene to their male offspring. Males have only one X-chromosome and the paired and shorter Y-chromosome does not carry a homologous gene at the appropriate position on the chromosome. If they are unfortunate enough to inherit the recessive gene, then colour blindness results.

The nature of the colour blindness depends upon whether the gene for the red-sensitive, green-sensitive or blue-sensitive pigment in the retinal cone cells is affected. Defective red-sensitive cone cells (photoreceptors) in the retina, whose light-sensitive pigment is non-functional or reduced in quantity, are the probable cause of protonopia, *ie* a relative insensitivity to red. Protonopes comprise some 1% of the male population, although 6% of the normal population of trichromats match colours with abnormal proportions of each of the primary colours, red, green and blue. My own case as tested with Ishihara Test Cards suggests a relatively strong protonopia, *ie* deficiency in the red light sensitive pigment. One of the peculiarities of red–green deficiencies is that blue–yellow colours appear to be remarkably clear compared with red and green colours. In protonopia the visible range of the spectrum is shorter at the red end compared to normal subjects; dark reds may be seen as black. The whole visible range of the spectrum in protonopia consists of two areas which are separated from each other by a grey part. Each area appears as one system of colour with different brightness and saturation. Partial defects produce protanomalia in which a part of the spectrum appears as a greyish indistinct colour.

My Ishihara Card results suggest either a protonopia or a protanomalia, a condition present neither in my Uncle John nor my cousin Tony Pearman, another grandson of Herbert Culpin, nor probably in my Uncle Frank (who received only a Y-chromosome from his father). The recessive gene for colour blindness was probably brought into the Culpin family by Eliza Matthews, the wife of BEL Culpin. She was the daughter of a Limerick man and sister of a veterinary surgeon. Since Eliza's children included Agnes, Walter, Ellen and Charlotte, as well as Ewart and Herbert Miall, the female children were inevitably carriers of the colour-blindness gene.

One of Nature's malign jokes is to provide a talent for art but couple it with a defect in colour vision. In my own case, a childhood precocity in art prompted thoughts of eventually reaching art school which were blighted by my colour blindness. I understood that this would automatically disqualify me from entry, but many years later discovered that some art schools, at least, are prepared to accept colour-blind students.

In evolution, the step to three types of colour-sensitive cone cell occurred rather late, perhaps only 30 million years ago. New World monkeys, just like me, have only two types of colour sensitivity, while Old World monkeys have three, and may safely be given a paintbrush. Perhaps my career might have taken a very different direction if I had gone to Art School, although I fancy my limited talent for painting would not have carried me very far. My daughter, I have been pleased to find, is a talented artist.

John Culpin died suddenly in 1974 at the age of 69, after a game of badminton. He had been playing at the Feathers Club, Letchworth, but after one game left the court. His friend found him slumped on the ground. His wife Sheila was not told of his death until 11 o'clock at night. She said: 'It was a terrible shock because my husband was such a keen sportsman.'

ETHNIE, GLADYS MADELEINE (GOLLY) AND EVELYN (MOLLY) (G-1)

Ethnie was the slightly plain one, Golly the pretty one and Molly the odd-ball amongst the Culpin daughters, with my mother Kathleen ranking somewhere in the middle of this spectrum. Ethnie was born in 1899, immeasurably kind, good-humoured and always ready to listen sympathetically to her nephews. Her parents were on holiday at Gorleston where they met someone with the name Ethnie and decided to use it to name their first daughter. Ethnie started work as a clerk at King's Cross station and then became a clerk at a garage and later at a leather company. In 1924 she married Bill Pearman whom she had met at a dance in Hitchin. They are pictured together in the early days of their marriage. Ethnie and Bill had two children who died in infancy (John and Mary) before Tony (Anthony William) was born in 1931. My Uncle Bill was an 'ideal Uncle' with a tweedy tobacco-ey jacket, a great aptitude for growing fruit and vegetables, a facility with chickens and one of those under-powered puttering motorbikes which took him on his rounds as a collector of weekly insurance payments. On his allotment in open stony ground, he would grow superb chrysanthemums, robust sweet peas, grafted roses and red lettuces of great sweetness. His garden meandered downhill from the house with cordoned apple and pear trees along the legs of the garden path towards two sheds of chickens. The lower shed was a cosy wooden affair with plenty of clean straw for his nesting birds. I learnt to remove the eggs from beneath the mildy protesting hens and to ignore

Grandfather Culpin and his siblings

Fig 40 – Ethnie Culpin and her mother and unidentified friend

their feeble pecks. Ill-health sneaked up on him at far too young an age and Ethnie was left to expend her great energy on perpetual jaunts, summer schools and country dancing sessions with my mother.

Gladys Madeleine seems never to have been referred to by this name but always Golly, probably because of her curly black hair. Auntie Golly, a woman suffused with maternal solicitude and gaiety, moved north to Newcastle with her five children. She had married Arthur Bray, something of a charmer, who was rarely much around during their Stevenage days. The wedding photograph (*Fig 43*) shows them outside the Bunyan Baptist Church in Basils Road, just a few yards away from her parents' house. The bridal attendants were Arthur's sister on the left of the photo and Molly Culpin next to the bride. Their five children were John, Alan, twins Bill and Diana, and Ethnie. Golly was divorced from Arthur Bray sometime

Fig 41 – Ethnie and Bill Pearman in about 1950

during the 1960s and re-married. She died around 1985, her second husband having predeceased her.

Evelyn Culpin or Molly was the youngest child of Herbert Miall and Kate. Unmarried, she progressed through stages of eccentricity to live eventually as a kind of hermit in a dilapidated cottage at the end of Letchmore Road, which she eventually signed over to her lodger. She was surrounded by unstable piles of bric-à-brac and many cats. In her youth, she had been a land-girl and worked as a gardener; indeed she had a talent for growing alpine plants and was very proud of her rockery in the front of 5 Basils Road. There was a second rockery in the back garden, the

Fig 42 – Golly (left front) and my mother (right back) at Guide Camp (with 'Auntie Eva', front right) in 1926

plants mainly being obtained from Clarence Elliott's Six Hills Nurseries. Molly had a strange swarthy complexion plentifully supplemented by moles but was not without a black, sarcastic sense of humour. Perhaps her excessive misanthropy was the result of being the youngest of a large family, the butt of her elder siblings and without sufficient charm to encourage admirers. Although in her later years she went out rather little, she was still brought by car to family gatherings at Christmas, at weddings and funerals. But even her charitable sisters could not resist the occasional faintly malicious gibe at her expense; there was something in their relationship which prompted this response.

Fig 43 – Golly and Arthur Bray on their wedding day photographed outside the Bunyan Baptist Church in Basils Road. Molly Culpin stands to the right of the bride

KATHLEEN MURIEL CULPIN (G-1)

My mother lived in Stevenage all her life until her death in 1991. It was her vigorous love of life which prompted these reminiscences of Stevenage past. Kathleen Wallis née Culpin surfaces many times in this history and her connections with the Wallis family figure in the next chapter. She was born in 1906 and educated at Hitchin Girls' Grammar School; she began to work for the Civil Service in 1923 calculating the interest in the National Savings Certificates Office. During the General Strike of 1926, when the trains stopped running early in the afternoon, she had to rush to catch a bus to the station in order to be in time for the last train home. There were then 'pirate' buses plying for trade and she slipped off one of these, breaking her nose and cutting her chin. She was taken by ambulance to the Royal National Hospital, kept in overnight and had to take time off work to recover. She went to convalesce at her grandparents' house in Battle. It was by remembering this event that mum knew her grandparents were still alive in 1926. In 1930 Kathleen married Leonard Stephen Wallis and gave up her civil service job to look after the house at 98 Fairview Road and bring up her family.

8

THE WALLIS FAMILY

Grandfather William Wallis must have moved from Dorset around the turn of the century. His father, my great-grandfather Richard Wallis, was at the 1881 Census a police constable of 38 living in Frampton, Dorset. Richard's mother was Susan Wallis of Owermoigne, Dorset, born in the nearby village of East Lulworth. She may have been a dressmaker. Richardís birth, registered at Portland for 28 October 1842, records him as being born at Reforne, Portland, father unknown, but he was baptised three years later in Owermoigne. Mary Hinde was present at the birth. In the 1851 Census Susan and Richard (aged 8) are included in the return for Owermoigne. Susan later married Charles E Way, a general dealer, of Bryantspuddle, Dorset. By 1881 Susan Way (aged 69) was living with Charles in Bryantspuddle, together with a border, Albert E Wallis, aged four.

Parish records and census returns show that Susan was one of a largish family of Wallises living in this small Dorset village a few miles south east of Dorchester. Weymouth is a similar distance away to the south west. No bastardy orders served on Richard's natural father have come to light, but as her parents took her in there was probably no need for court intervention.

Susan's parents, John and Martha (née Penney) were married in East Lulworth, a village near the coast and the beauty spot of Lulworth Cove, on 20 August 1811, both recorded as residents of this parish. The witnesses were William Wallis and Juliana Slade. John Wallis was an agricultural labourer, although later in life he is listed as the sub-Postmaster for Owermoigne. The family seems to have moved to Owermoigne soon after Susan's sisters, Martha, Elizabeth and Rebecca were born. All three were baptised in Owermoigne. The trail further back from John Wallis is more tentative. He was 64 years of age at the time of the 1851 census, and probably baptised in East Lulworth on 26 November 1786 to Daniel and Elizabeth Wallis. There were a number of Wallis families in the area. Two other such families were baptising children at that time – Revd Samuel and Mary Wallis, and James and Mary Wallis. Assuming Daniel, born 1756, was John's father, then Daniel's father was probably a further John Wallis born some time around 1730 but not baptised in Owermoigne. Several of Daniel's siblings – John, Elizabeth,

If I were a Blackbird ...

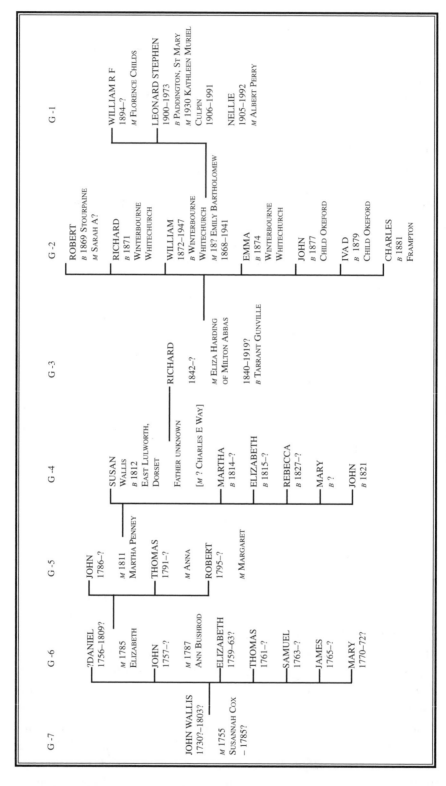

Fig 44 – Wallis family tree

Thomas, Samuel, James and Mary – were baptised in Owermoigne in the period 1757 to 1770 *(see Fig 44)*.

The village of Owermoigne has thatched cottages with whitewashed walls which surround the old parish church. Its population was 400 in 1891 and only 433 in 1991. Owermoigne was originally a Saxon settlement called Ogre or later Oweres. The name appears to have been the result of linking this name with that of the Norman Lords of the Manor, the Le Moignes. The Moignes or Moygnes lived in the area for 300 years, and also gave their name to Shipton Moyne in Gloucestershire. The parish church of St Michael's stands at the heart of the village whose first recorded Rector was Walter Chaundos (1333). The living was in the patronage of John Le Moigne.

RICHARD WALLIS

Great-grandfather Richard married Eliza Harding, three years older than him. She had been born in Tarrant Gunville, Dorset. By 1881 they had seven children born in various small villages in Dorset, apparently because Richard, as a village policeman, was regularly moved from village to village *(see Fig 44)*. Robert Wallis was born in 1869 at Stourpaine, Richard in 1871 at Winterborne Whitechurch, William on 15 July 1872 at Winterborne Whitechurch or Milton Abbas, also Emma in 1874, John in 1877 at Child Okeford, Iva (Francis) D in 1879 at Child Okeford and Charles in 1881 at Frampton. Great-grandfather subsequently became a sergeant in the Dorset police.

By 1901 Richard and Eliza had moved on his retirement to the village of Shillingstone, Dorset. The family had become widely dispersed. Robert became a grocer in Wolverhampton, John (Jack) became a railway shunter in Notttingham and later a London policeman, Charles (Charlie) was living as a lodger with Alfred Sparks in Bournemouth and worked as Bootmaker Improver. Emma was still living with her parents but worked as a cook and Iva, also living at home, worked at a butter factory.

WILLIAM (1872–1947) AND EMILY WALLIS (1868–1941)

Grandfather William, born in Milton Abbas near Winterborne Whitechurch, appears to have moved to London and subsequently to Stevenage. He worked for many years as a compositor at the Stevenage Printing Works in the High Street. William married Emily Bartholomew five years his elder. In the Census for 1901 they are living at 192 Bravington Rd, Paddington, with their two sons William (Uncle Bill), aged 7, and Leonard aged 4 months. In Stevenage they lived in a smallish house at 31 Green Street. Emily and William, as well as their two sons Bill and Leonard, had a daughter Nellie. They can all be seen in the wedding

Fig 45 – Bill and Flo's Wedding. Grandpa Wallis is on the far left, Grandma Wallis on the far left of the front row

photograph of my Uncle Bill and Florence Childs (Auntie Flo), dating from some time in the twenties. Auntie Flo was audibly cockney; they lived in Croxley Green in the outer suburbs of London. Mum visited them once travelling by bus from St Albans. My Grandma's broad face can be seen mirrored in those of both Bill and Nellie. She is wearing shiny black boots and a fur-trimmed coat. Later in life Grandma Wallis became a little, slightly frail old lady with white hair. We saw very little of Bill and Flo. One of the few occasions when the Stevenage Wallises went to

Fig 46 – Bill and Flo on their wedding day

see them was on their Silver Wedding, when a somewhat raucous party was thrown, drink flowed, and dad looked a little down his nose at the goings-on, particularly those of the flamboyant Flo and her relatives. Flo's parents are probably the couple on the extreme right of the photograph. Bill and the sharp-featured but good-natured Flo can be seen in another photograph from around this time. Bill was a shortish man with a broad forehead and his father-in-law the possessor of formidable mutton-chop whiskers. Sadly, Bill took to drink late in life after Flo died. My dad reckoned he consumed two bottles of whisky a day.

Fig 47 – Bill later in life

LEONARD AND NELLIE PERRY, NÉE WALLIS

The birth of Leonard Stephen Wallis was registered at St Mary's, Paddington, Sub-District on 7 January 1901 recorded as 26 November 1900. Leonard married Kathleen Muriel Culpin, whose birth was registered by C Stuart Toll in the Baldock Sub-District of Hitchin for 5 June 1906. Kathleen and Len came from different non-conformist congregations in Stevenage where most people knew each other, but most were highly conscious of class boundaries. To go to the local Grammar School, for instance, was a mark of privilege – and a question of money before the Education Bill established the Eleven-Plus Exam and free grammar school education after the war.

My Auntie Nellie also married someone from Stevenage – Albert Perry. Neither my Dad nor my Uncle Albert had been to Stevenage (Alleyne's) Grammar School but had been educated at Letchmore Road

Boys' School. Both joined the clerical staff of the LNER (London and North Eastern Railway) but Uncle Albert managed to progress much further up the hierarchy. Dad, I think, knew that Albert was more ambitious, more upwardly mobile than himself. And yet Leonard had married into a family considerably more prosperous than his own, his father-in-law a civil servant in the Admiralty and one of the car-owning élite. Both mum and dad were sometimes over-concerned about the opinions of people they viewed as belonging to social strata above their own. Uncle Albert had more assurance and a jolly confidence that was reinforced with a slight northern accent.

Uncle Albert and my father pose as 'likely lads' in a photograph of them in their twenties. Looking as if dressed for tennis, Uncle Albert and Auntie Nellie in a seaside photograph are happy and relaxed, ready for a long life of secure contentment. For many years they lived at 16 Bridge Road, a field's walk away to Green Street and William and Emily Wallis, reached by a swing gate, steps and a footpath. It was on this footpath that my father and I met Uncle Albert belatedly one lunchtime in 1941. Grandma Wallis had had a heart attack early in the morning on Monday, 1 September, and died two days later, and Albert had been at the Green Street house helping his father-in-law to sort things out. 'You dirty rat' he hissed at dad, the only unkind words I heard, or was ever to hear, him speak. Dad turned round and walked back to Fairview Road.

Bill and Flo came to Stevenage for the funeral. Grandpa Wallis left Green Street and the house was sold. In gradually deteriorating health he lived until 1947, either staying with us in Fairview Road or with his daughter in Bridge Road. It was there, as the funeral notice shows, that he died suddenly on 13 May 1947 at the end of a fiercely harsh winter and during the worst rigours of post-war austerity. He is buried with Emily in the churchyard at St Nicholas Church, Stevenage. Like my father, he had a good bass-baritone voice. They both sang for many years in the choir of the Stevenage Methodist Church. Grandpa Wallis was a local preacher on the Methodist Circuit. My mother notes in her diaries that he preached at Stevenage on 6 August 1944.

SIXTEEN BRIDGE ROAD

Sixteen Bridge Road was a warmly welcoming house and always more comfortable than our own. My brother and I stayed there on a number of occasions and frequently visited our cousins, Janet and Marilyn, daughters of Nellie and Albert. The house was in an attractive location because over the road were grass tennis courts in a walled area behind the White Lion Pub. In post-war years, the courts survived as an increasingly uneconomic private tennis club, with probably the best grass surface for

Fig 48 – Dad and Uncle Albert as 'likely lads'

miles around. My father and I always made a ritual visit to Bridge Road on Christmas Eve, when cards and presents were delivered and exchanged for Christmas Day. On Christmas Day itself, the Wallises went off to join the assembled Culpins in Basils Road and the Perrys, I think, went off to join their family. Rosy with anticipation of the day to come, the Christmas Eve visit seemed a particularly happy occasion. It would be misleading to say 'drink was partaken' for, though it certainly was by Nellie and Albert, Methodist Abstentionism dictated non-alcoholic liquid for dad. He and I both had glasses of Stones' Ginger Wine whose charms were much enhanced by the occasion. Nellie and Albert later moved to live in London and, after Albert's retirement, to the south coast near Eastbourne.

Fig 49 – Albert and Nellie at the seaside

The sensitivities of post-war England and of a small provincial town to social class allowed an acute awareness of the standing of the regular congregants of the Stevenage Methodist Church. Nellie and Albert were not amongst those, for they attended erratically and not often. The majority of Stevenage Methodists seemed to comprise a very few businessmen, one or two local farmers, a number of shopkeepers and relatively large numbers of commuting clerical workers. Very few belonged to the poorest kinds of working families, such as manual labourers, farm workers, factory workers or domestic servants. The generally held view was, I suspect, that these would be more happily accommodated by the Revivalist Chapels in the town. Perhaps the gradually increasing numbers of factory workers were uninterested in

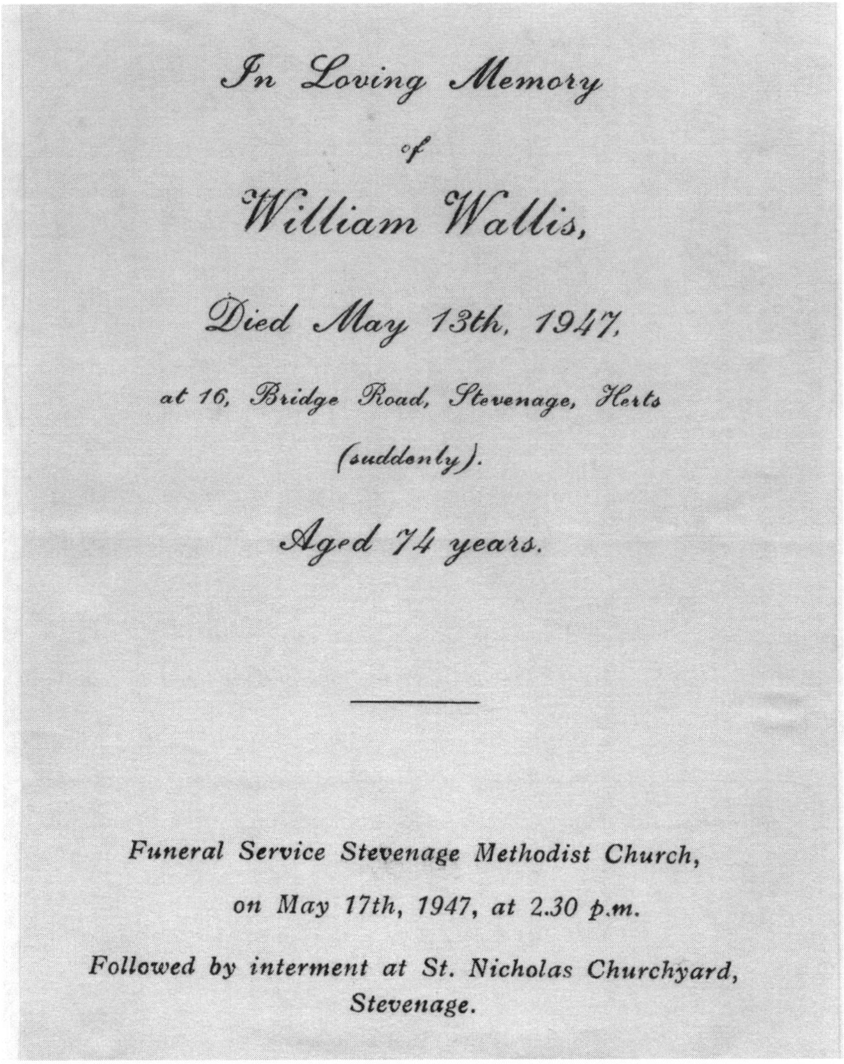

In Loving Memory

of

William Wallis,

Died May 13th, 1947,

at 16, Bridge Road, Stevenage, Herts

(suddenly).

Aged 74 years.

―――――――

Funeral Service Stevenage Methodist Church,

on May 17th, 1947, at 2.30 p.m.

Followed by interment at St. Nicholas Churchyard,
Stevenage.

Fig 50 – Funeral Notice for William Wallis

either religion or in the kind of religion provided by the Stevenage Methodist Church. Did this account for a certain lack of vigour in our church? Is it significant that Methodism has seen the need to re-invent itself by creating 'missions' to such realms of the ungodly as Stevenage and its surrounds?

LEONARD WALLIS, KATHLEEN WALLIS AND THEIR CHILDREN

Kate and Herbert Miall Culpin issued invitations to their daughter Kathleen's wedding at the Bunyan Baptist Church, Basils Road Stevenage, and afterwards at 'Elstow' Basils Road. The marriage certificate was signed by Alfred Enoch Phillips, Minister of the Bunyan Baptist Church, for 5 July 1930. Leonard Stephen Wallis, 29, Railway

If I were a Blackbird ...

Fig 51 – Mum and Dad about the time of their wedding

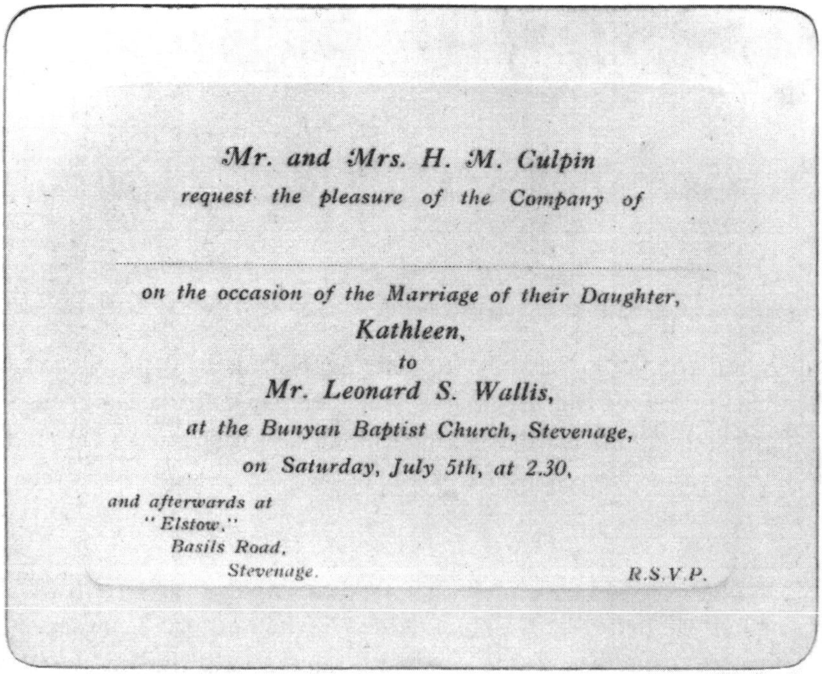

Mr. and Mrs. H. M. Culpin
request the pleasure of the Company of

on the occasion of the Marriage of their Daughter,
Kathleen,
to
Mr. Leonard S. Wallis,
at the Bunyan Baptist Church, Stevenage,
on Saturday, July 5th, at 2.30,
and afterwards at
" Elstow,"
Basils Road,
Stevenage.   R.S.V.P.

Fig 52 – Wedding Invitation (1930)

The Wallis Family

Fig 53 – Wedding Group

Clerk, married Kathleen Muriel Culpin, 24, Clerical Officer Civil Service, the fathers' names were recorded and the witnesses were Emily Wallis and H M Culpin. According to the local press, 'the wedding was of considerable interest to Stevenage residents, many of whom were present at the church. The bride is closely associated with the Girl Guide and Sunday School movements. The bride, who was given away by her father, wore a gown of ivory crepe de Chine, with a long skirt, with godets, finished with a belt and diamante buckle. Her veil was held in place with a wreath of orange blossom and she carried a shower bouquet of white and pink roses and wore a pearl necklace. There were two bridesmaids, Miss G M Culpin, sister of the bride (on the right in *Fig 53*), and Miss N Wallis, sister of the bridegroom. The bridesmaids wore sleeveless gowns and coatees of flowered silk georgette with a peach ground. They wore wreaths of gold leaves and rosebuds, and carried bouquets of peach roses. The many presents included a gift from the Wesleyan and Bunyan churches, and a canteen of cutlery from the goods' managers office, King's Cross, where the bridegroom is employed. After the reception Mr and Mrs Wallis left for Dunoon where the honeymoon is being spent. The bride's travelling dress was of brown flowered silk with a tweed coat and hat to match.'

Fig 54 – Rates Office Liverpool Street Station. Dad is partly obscured by the lady telephoning in the foreground

Dad used to travel to London every day by train to work in various offices of the LNER, first at Marylebone in central London and during the war, at Woodford where the office was evacuated. By 1961, after Nationalisation, he was working in the Rates Office, Room 74, General Offices of Eastern Region at Liverpool Street. The picture (*Fig 54*) was issued by their Public Relations and Publicity Officer and suggests a kind of cloistered calm probably very far from the true atmosphere in the office, which often prompted a moan or two from my dad. Working on the railway provided the perk of a number of rail passes and privilege tickets for dad and the family during the course of the year. We would use these to go on holiday and make trips to London. Even during the war my mother's diary notes a trip to the Houndsditch Warehouse, near the City, to purchase a coat and blazer for me. Later, we went to the Thames Embankment to take a tour of Captain Scott's ship, *Discovery*. Another treat had been a visit to Madame Tussauds and the Chamber of Horrors.

Dad not only sang in the Methodist church choir which occasionally joined local choirs to perform oratorios, but at social events gave a solo turn. He was particularly fond of sentimental Victorian Ballads involving 'roaming' and being a 'rover' or an 'adventurer' of which he was neither. Once or twice, he entered talent competitions in London – at a Finsbury Park cinema, he sang 'Old Father Thames' and won second prize. Fame and fortune did not follow and the prize was a munificent twelve shillings and six-pence. Two of his favourites were 'The Glad Highway':

The glad day breaking on the road you're taking

And the world a land of song.

That's the hour you cherish, for your cares all perish

As you gaily march along.

The skies above you seem to kiss and love you,

And the big winds wander by,

In this world so weary there's no life so cheery

As a roving life, say I! *etc*

And 'Wandering the King's Highway':

I've always been a rover, summer and winter too,

Wandering the wide world over,

Tramping the wide world through.

But when I start my journey, at the dawn of another day

I give a health to comrades,

Pals of the Great Highway.

So long to you, got to be on the road again,

So long to you, got to hitch up my load again,

It's been great to meet you here

Right good company and right good cheer;

Now then, my lads ! Anyone like to come with me?

A wand'rer's life is free,

I can say, Night and Day, nothing ever worries me

Wandering the King's Highway, *etc.*

And on frequent occasions a song totally in keeping with the townsman's view of rural life: 'Leanin':

Sowin's pretty good, reapin ain't so bad,

Scarin of the crows suits a farmer's lad,

But if you ax-es me

The thing that suits a feller

Is a little bit of straw to suck

To keep your fancies meller

When you're leanin on the gate beside the pond

That lies beside the side of farmer's stack of new mown hay.

It's just a twix the ricks beside the barn

Where farmer sticks inside the chicks he only hatched today.

Leanin, lean-in. I'm champion down our way, they say!

At lean-in on the gate beside the pond that lies

Beside the side of farmer's stacks of new mown hay

That he's been gleanin, while I've been leanin

All day.

And continues:

> Had a lurcher once. Better than a gal.
> Poacher? Well a bit, but 'e was a pal.
> Now there's just a mound underneath the ell-um
> Reck-on folks would laff at oi
> If I was tell 'em
> Why I'm leanin on the gate beside the pond
> That lies beside the side the hedge where
> My old dog would play, *etc.*

Dad also sang, although not so frequently, 'The Harvester's Night Song' and 'The Blind Ploughman'. He left 'Bless this House' and 'I'll walk beside you' to contraltos of a certain age.

The attraction of the open road was 'of its time', a characteristic attitude to a supposedly once-existing opportunity to roam the British countryside unencumbered by practical matters such as earning a living to provide for your family. My father may have felt particularly constrained by the conventions of suburban small-town life, the limited imaginative horizons and a surviving class consciousness which prevented people from departing from their 'station in life', but, if he did, he kept such thoughts to himself.

My father can be seen, aged 36, pushing me along the Prom of some breezy South Coast resort, mum and Auntie Ethnie lagging slightly behind. In another picture on a trip to the seaside, probably Hunstanton around 1946 or 1947, the family poses for the camera (*see Fig 56)*. My younger brother, Graham, stands on the left and in the background can be seen Grandpa Culpin's Standard car. Grandpa presumably took the photograph. At that time my mother must have been around 40. She lived a good Christian life, loved us all and her neighbour as herself, and even to the end displayed incredible energy and an inquiring mind. Probably children were cuddled less in those days, but she adored kids and was totally at ease playing with them. In a last photograph she sits, in old age, in her back living room at 98 Fairview Road. The clock that she and dad were given as a wedding present stands on the bureau beside the picture of our old chocolate-coloured cocker spaniel, 'Brownie'.

Saturday Morning Shopping

On Saturday morning Dad and I would do weekend shopping – meat and groceries had usually been bought during the week. Memories of the High Street shops in the Forties and Fifties have been refreshed by 'The changing face of Stevenage High Street 1837–1997'[25].

The Wallis Family

Fig 55 – A South Coast Sunny Snap

Fig 56 – A day trip to Hunstanton

Fig 57 – Mum in old age

Dad was a pipe smoker for much of his life until he was obliged to stop for health reasons. Our first stop was for pipe tobacco at the shop at the bottom of Bridge Road (58 High Street). Chelsom's tobacconists was an ancient shop, entered via a set of steps, whose character was somewhat spoilt by being modernised into antiquity by a subsequent owner. The rustic appearance of the place was no doubt partly due to its previous incarnation as a saddlers, run by Mr Gentle in the 1870s, and before that as a Haybinders, proprietor in 1861 Mr. Thomas Furr. Furr was a famous Stevenage name. By wartime and after, Furr's Fish Shop at 97 High Street had declined from its prior grandeur of rows upon rows of pheasants, partridge, grouse and hares towards a late-night fish-and-chip shop, 'Fishy Furrs'. In 1949, his adverts still hinted at past splendours: G M Furr, Fish Merchant, Poulterer, Game Dealer, *etc* – Deliveries daily, prompt attention, Haddocks cured on the premises!

By 1955 the tobacconist's was run by Mr. Depienne. During the war, the shop still sold the old and cheap clay pipes used at that time by pensioners and certain schoolboys, all of whom should have known a deal better. Schoolboys were also known to buy Woodbine cigarettes there. From time to time, dad would get his tobacco from another shop just a few doors along, at 52A High Street, Sayers-Clarke, Tobacconist and Confectioner. Upstairs there was a barber's shop which sometimes did my hair and, at the back, a small lending library.

Fig 58 – Chamber's Library. Drawing from a photograph in The Book of Stevenage *(courtesy Margaret Ashby)*

Dad and I then proceeded south along the High Street, unless a trip to Woolworth's (50 High Street) or a look in Mr Hawkes' shoe shop at No 30 was required (H G Hawkes, Scientific Shoe Fitter, Shoes fitted by X-Ray). Mr Hawkes probably had passed on to him shoe making tools from the previous owners, Miss Lizzie Goldfinch (in the 1930s) and Culpin and son, Boot and Shoe Shop, who occupied the premises from the 1880s. This Culpin was my great-uncle Wallie (Wallace or Walter) Culpin, who was Herbert Miall's brother. The Culpins seem to have occupied the shop in 1914 and 1904, but in the 1870s it had been a butcher's, occupied by W Moulden. Mr Moulden probably moved from 32 High Street, later to become Bickell's watch shop.

Dad usually had to get a loaf or two, and sometimes buns, at F J Hart, Baker and Confectioner at 64 High Street, still showing signs of operating as a café. My dad normally had business at the Bank and would call at Barclay's Branch at 68 High Street. This branch was already operating in 1904. Just beyond the bank, H J Horsnell ran a thriving confectioner's shop at 72 High Street. His son Reg had been my near contemporary at school and eventually took over the shop from his substantially rotund father. Although this shop is still recorded for 1978, by 1989 it had disappeared, at least as a confectioner's.

Chamber's Library, also the *Hertfordshire Express* Newspaper Office, stood on the corner at 61–63 High Street. This half-timbered building was our weekly source of the *Radio Times, John Bull* and *Woman's Own*. They also sold sweets, perhaps a hangover from the days in 1914 when the shop had been H J Chambers, Confectioners, and were a great source of knitting patterns. By 1978 it had become the 'Stevenage Gazette Office' and by 1989 an Estate Agent's. In 1946, it advertised as 'The Leading Newsagents, Hundreds of satisfied Customers, Delivery service covers all parts of Stevenage and Wymondley: Office Requisites, Fancy Goods, Toys, Wools, Mendings, Travel Linen, Transfers, etc.'

If painting and decorating were to be done there was a choice. My dad would keep half-full and half-solid pots of paint in his garden shed, together with jars of brushes in various stages of fossilisation, just waiting to be cleaned up for future use. But touching up the paintwork and creosoting the fence and the sheds were occasionally unavoidable, although these jobs were eventually delegated to me. Lines Ironmonger's shop at 76 High Street on the corner of Green Street was an Aladdin's Cave selling an intriguing mix which ranged from clothes pegs, paint brushes and paints, tools of all sorts, through to fireworks. The shop has survived to 2005, having been in existence since at least 1937, and having previously been James Silk, Ironmonger, from 1904 or so. A compressed version of Lines shop suddenly appeared sometime after the war on the opposite side of the road. This was J Deamers, Hardware, China and Glass, at 67 High Street, which also survived until 2005.

We would get fruit and veg, although dad grew a good deal himself, from Nichols' shop at 75 High Street. W G Nichols' advert from the Stevenage Guide for 1946 doesn't say, but might have done, that home delivery was on offer. For a while I was the frequently cold and wet errand boy pedalling the heavy bike that held a box of greengroceries in its front pannier. The piece of cake and glass of juice I received at the

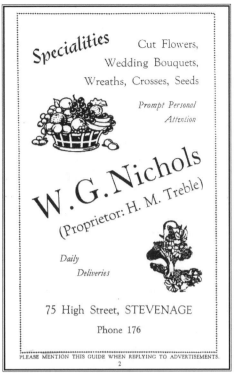

Specialities Cut Flowers, Wedding Bouquets, Wreaths, Crosses, Seeds

Prompt Personal Attention

W. G. Nichols
(Proprietor: H. M. Treble)

Daily Deliveries

75 High Street, STEVENAGE

Phone 176

PLEASE MENTION THIS GUIDE WHEN REPLYING TO ADVERTISEMENTS.
2

Fig 59 – Advertisement for Nichols' Shop 1946

point of delivery eased the pain, but the whole thing was too much for an indulged eleven-year old to sustain for long. Nichols' Greengrocers had superseded W A Croft, Greengrocers, who operated from the same premises in 1914 and 1904. By 1955, 75 High Street had become a dry cleaners and by 1997 part of 'Fourboys' Newsagents and Food.

As I passed through my teens, trousers and jackets would be bought from a Gents' Outfitter's shop, Beales and Larman, located at 89 High Street. Before the war this had been a tailor's (V Croft) and prior to that a butcher's, but has now mutated into an Electrical Goods Store. In 1949 the proprietor had been a Mr H Swannell, who advertised himself as 'Gentleman's Outfitters – Worsted Flannels, Sport Coats, Summer Sports Wear, Suits, Harris, Donegal and West of England Tweeds. Dou Yo [sic] wear McKay Shirts? – The shirt of Quality and Style.'

A shop fascinating to boys, due to its mass display of bicycles, sets of Meccano, Hornby trains and hidden fireworks, was the cycle agent's T W & E O Boorman at 115 High Street. Perhaps my memories are pre-war because during wartime it must have been severely depleted of stock. The shop was already a cycle agents in 1914 (Bookers), but previously had been the premises of Mr F S Higgins, Chemist, Dentist and Artificial

Teeth Maker, perhaps a premonitory sign of its current transmogrification into 'Perfect Pizza, Take-away'. To reach Boormans' we had to pass the Stevenage Printing Works at 109 High Street where Grandad Wallis used to work.

We usually had no occasion to call at two shops on the other side of the High Street, but frequent visits with my mother, and the striking character of these establishments, have left vivid memories. The butchers, Farmers and Graziers, had a sawdust-covered floor and a booth in which sat the cashier. Animals for slaughter were driven out of lorries through the driveway north of Jones Grocers' yard into the backyard and slaughter shed, dramatically careening down this narrow passageway. Jones' shop (116 High Street) also had sawdust on the floor and all manner of dry goods in open sacks, wooden drawers, tins, boxes and bags. Mr Jones lived along Fairview Road and my brother and I were thick with his son Dennis. Beyond the backyard of the shop was a concreted area where we could play cricket and a dark, inviting warehouse whose interior emitted an entrancing mixture of smells of molasses, sultanas, dried apricots and figs. Up a set of wooden steps was a gallery where the more valuable goods were stored. Mr Jones had his own painted delivery lorries manufactured, appropriately, by Dennis. There was a Wine and Spirits Shop also belonging to Mr Jones at 120 High Street. Jones the Grocers had been there since 1914, superseding an earlier grocery establishment of Mr Wright and before that a Mr Herbert Titmuss, Corndealer. The rich smells have not gone away as the premises became in 1978 or so 'La Concho D'Oro Restaurant' and then 'Mohan Tandoori Restaurant'. Farmers and Graziers (118 High Street) had previously been a butchers (Ashwells), but in more recent times (1978) had swept away the sawdust to become Anglia Sound & Vision and subsequently Countryside & Camping, also Ski and Climbing Equipment.

THE CINEMAS

The two Stevenage Cinemas were contrasts in style. The Publix Cinema overlooking the Bowling Green had a mock Tudor upper storey and had been converted from a private house or business premises. On the High Street Plan for 1923, it is shown as the Cinema Picture House. According to Abercrombie's 'Greater London Plan' *(see Fig 21)*: 'The cinema, faced with badly designed sham half-timber work, terminates the main street vista to the north.' The upper-most seats, sought after by courting teenagers, were cramped and in a narrow section just under the projection box. This projector was much given to mechanical failure. The Publix was the home of Comedy Shorts, especially Laurel and Hardy, and American Westerns. 'They died with their boots on' lodges in the memory, together with some film in which Alan Ladd played a diver and wrestled with a giant squid, while on deck ladies in frilly skirts fretted over him. As Margaret Ashby remarks in her book[8], the Publix lacked refinements. Its seats, originally bolted to the floor, soon came apart, and the springs poked through the covers; a corrugated iron hut outside housed the lavatories.

The Astonia was concrete barn-style at the bottom of Pound Avenue, just beyond the old Workhouse. This was the town's modern cinema so that the most recent, popular Hollywood films were shown there. My mother's diary records us going to see, together with our evacuee Dora, *The Wizard of Oz* on 12 November, 1940, and *Dumbo* on 9 August 1943, followed by *Bambi* on the 30 August the same year. The Astonia was converted to a Bingo Hall which was in turn shut down in 1982.

STEVENAGE FAIR

Each autumn Stevenage Charter Fair transformed the High Street to create a brief carnival. Edward I had granted a charter in 1281 to hold an annual three-day Fair on the eve, the day and the morrow of the Feast of St John the Baptist (23–25 June). The days have since been changed to 22 and 23 September, but the Fair has continued for over 700 years. The original intentions were as much to do with trade as with entertainment, an occasion to hire servants and sell horses and other livestock. The fair booths and rides were set up along the High Street from Trinity Church to the corner of Hitchin Road with many of the larger attractions being accommodated in Franklin's Field (see 8). There was no Fair as such during the years of the Second World War, although some members of the Fairmans' Guild kept a stall in the High Street to maintain their right under law to hold the fair. A return of the jazzy festivities was eagerly awaited during the grey, utility years of rationing after the war. Though some sighed at the noise and disruption there was no posting of warning notices, such as the town had seen in the 1930s, which warned of prosecution for the 'selling or using of water squirts' and for 'damaging the turf, *etc* on the Greens in the town, by cutting, burning or in any other way'[8]. Rather, the roundabouts, coconut shies, swing boats, the cake-walk, the gondolas, the chair-o-planes and any number of stalls, the brash music and harsh voices of the fair people, greatly increased the 'gaiety of nations and enriched the public stock of harmless pleasure' to adapt Dr Johnson.

THE BOXING BOOTH

Franklin's Field was the site of most of the newer and larger rides, as well as some of the more traditional booths. I can remember a Freak Show tent with its Bearded Lady and Pituitary Dwarves, long extinct of political correctness, and a 'Test-your-strength' machine, where passing galants were invited to show their strength by striking with a sledge-hammer a peg connected to a pulley and weight. Correct application of the hammer, requiring both brute force and skill, would zoom the weight upwards along a track to ring a bell at the top of the device.

The key attraction for me was the Boxing Booth. This was a large tent with a small stage in front and a painted wooden surround, whose folk art depicted behemoths of old in vivid action. On the stage, the owner in bow tie and shabby dinner jacket and, perforce, the master of ceremonies, referee and principal hustler, would address the crowd with the aid of a microphone. Skipping or wanly shadow-boxing beside him would be two of the booth boxers, often somewhat long-in-the-tooth and over-weight, and not too keen on the skipping. The assembled populace would be invited to take on a booth fighter of their choice and win a crisp new fiver if they could last three rounds. And, of course, some there would be, anxious for the money, generally farms lads or local toughs keen to show their strength, lacking in boxing skills, ready to be persuaded to take up the challenge. They would later appear kitted out and ready to make ill-timed rushes and launch bludgeoning hay-makers at the booth fighter. There were no push-overs. The Proprietor had carefully weighed up the ineptitude of his volunteer against the decayed skills of his own fighter. One or two of the latter would show signs of impaired motor co-ordination, a hint of punchiness in their robotic programming. He offered each contender 'easy money', but 'would not promise to pay one single copper coin' if he failed to last 'three short rounds'.

The booth boxers would woozily bob and weave and fend off the eager young challenger, bloodying a nose here or delivering a solid cuff as an occasional deterrent. Most challengers survived the three rounds though visibly the worse for wear and, though sometimes knocked down, they were rarely knocked out. The more interesting fights would be between a war veteran and a booth boxer. One veteran was smallish, moustachioed, as if he might have served in the RAF. His trunks and boxing boots, clearly his own, were shabby and faded, as if long and draining campaigns had bleached the pigment from them. Another was taller, more haggard, scraggy and anxious-looking, somewhat unwell. In the ring, he moved with more assurance, blocked more blows, and his punches suggested an unexpected strength in scrawny arms. The booth boxers were more troubled by these challengers and the rules of engagement changed. The Proprietor gave the impression of having come across them before. He wagered that his own man would be on his feet after three rounds with the challenger. And the veterans could indeed punch. The booth boxer would ship punches, ride punches, hold, smother, stagger, take short counts, show alarming signs of his own mortality, but somehow survive to the final bell. The tall veteran had an excellent straight left and the booth boxer little answer to it; he took several short counts but spoiling tactics allowed him to be on his feet at the end, satisfying his paymaster if not the beery partisan crowd.

9

THE TOWN FOOTBALL CLUB

This chapter is dedicated to the memory of 'Lummy' Taylor.

Soon after turning right out of Chequers Bridge Road past the big houses in London Road, strains of 'If I were a blackbird' would be heard above the modest traffic. The football ground loudspeaker on a match day proclaimed:

> 'If I were a blackbird, I'd whistle and sing,
> And follow the ship that my true love sailed in
> And on the top rigging I'd there build my nest'

A necessary prelude to every game played by the Town in the years following the Second World War.

About a quarter of a mile along were the gates to the ground in a break in the hedgerow. There was a view across the ground to the other side of the main railway line and Geo King's factory. The grandstand and old changing rooms were just inside the hedge and close to the Great North (London) Road. During the war, we had come here from Letchmore Road Boys' School for football games and changed into our football boots sitting on the worn and creosoted timbers of the grandstand. A newer, brick changing room had been constructed besides the grandstand and, presumably providing better facilities, was used by the home side. Team photographs were often taken with the Town posed before it.

THE FIRST SEASON

On 19 September 1884 the football club had been formed at a meeting in the Town Hall attended by about twenty people. The Reverend William Jowitt, the Rector, was elected president, Mr H J Salmon of Highfield became captain, with a committee of W H Wadsworth, J Gillespie, F W Poland and T S Berry. The Hon Secretary and Treasurer was Mr P H Dunn. The *Stevenage Local Magazine* for October 1884 has it that kit would be 'black and amber caps (in halves) with white knickerbockers and shirts.' The first match was against Biggleswade in October and Stevenage lost 5–2. In the words of the *Magazine*: 'The visitors won the toss and having elected to start from the north end, soon obtained a goal from the foot of Mantle. Stevenage, however, were not slow to retaliate as a combined rush by P Dunn and Gilham and a good pass by the former resulted in R Dunn obtaining a goal, and shortly afterwards Bible again scored for the home team. The score remained unchanged till "half-time", after which Mantle, Cranfield and Styles obtained goals in quick succession, Cranfield kicking two; while Stevenage, though they now and again pressed their opponents, were unsuccessful in their shots. For the winners, Stubbs, Mantle, Colecome and Cranfield were most conspicuous, and for Stevenage Gilham, the brothers Dunn, and Hughes worked hard in front, while Nutting's back play was invaluable.

'Stevenage: T Ellis (goal), J B Nutting and A James (backs), J Kirk and T W S Berry (half-backs), F Gilham and Hughes (right wing), R Gilham, P Dunn (captain), and W Wadsworth (centre), R Dunn and S Bible (left wing). Umpire, Mr F Snooks.'

The team list thus appears to involve 12 players, one of whom was perhaps a Reserve or a Substitute. The fixtures for that first season were subsequently against Hitchin and St Neots, both home and away, Biggleswade away and Barnet and Hadley, home and away.

Fig 60 – The original Stripes of 1897 in their half-white, half-red shirts.
Back row, left to right: C Snow (Secretary), A Norman, W (Brock) Carpenter, P Wray (Captain), Mr Stanley (Referee); middle row : F Swannell, A Litchfield, L Blow; front : S Bird, E Albone, J Inns, E Preece, H Day. (Courtesy of Clive Abrey, Stevenage Borough FC).

THE STRIPES

Perhaps this all-white kit came across as too anaemic. By 1897 it had changed to half white, half red; by 1905 the striped shirts whose muddy endeavours linger fondly in the memory had been adopted and 'the stripes' remain today as the standard strip of Stevenage Borough Football Club.

The Town Club became an affiliated member of the Hertfordshire Football Association, initially competing in the North Herts League and local charity competitions. Simon Mortimer, Programme Editor for Stevenage Borough Football Club, has summarised their early history. The North Herts League Division One Championship was won in 1919–20, the team photograph appearing in *The Book of Stevenage*[8]. Unfortunately, neither players nor officials are identified. Fifteen players including the goalkeeper are present together with nine officials. Three cups are on display for what must have been a highly successful year for the club. During this period, many trophies were won including the Herts Charity Shield, Hitchin Hospital Cup, Letchworth Hospital Cup and Stevenage Hospital Cup. Stevenage were also winners of the League Division One in 1920–1 and the Premier Division title was gained in 1922–3 and again in 1931–2 (*see Fig 74 for the team*). The 1920–21 team with players, officials and their trophies appear in *Stevenage in Old Photographs*[12]. Between 1926 and 1932, the club had three spells in the South Midlands League and won the Division Two title in 1930–1, before moving by election to the Spartan League. Stevenage Town were runners up in Division Two East of the Spartan League before the Second World War, and were Division One runners up in 1947–8.

Fig 61 – The Stripes of 1920–21 which won the North Herts League Division title in 1921. Two Dymoke brothers played in the team; Christopher Dymoke is third from the left in the back row and Frank Dymoke third from right. (by kind permission from Stevenage Museum)

The Town Football Club

Fig 62 – The Stripes in 1947–48.
Back row, left to right : H Morris, P Atkins, E Scott, E Henderson, R Jones, P
Wilde, J Caldecote, V Folbigg, L Phillips; centre : F Chuck, K Watson, R
Abrahams; front : R Revell, B Johnson, A Jackson, Les Taylor, B Hudson.

PROMOTION TO THE DELPHIAN LEAGUE

Photographs from 1947 and 1950 are the earliest pictures available of two Stevenage heroes – Alan Jackson, the keystone of the defence, and the rumbustious and dashing forward 'Lummy' Taylor. Some of the pictures in this chapter have been taken from Lummy's scrapbook which he was kind enough to lend me in 2002, just before his death. I am greatly indebted to him and very grateful for the help provided by Mr Vic Folbigg, team manager for Stevenage Town in the 1950s.

In 1948–49, Stevenage Town were league champions and won promotion to the Premier Division of the Spartan League. Town teams from around 1950 are shown in two photographs. Alan Jackson and Lummy Taylor are in both, and Arthur Bloxham, Johnny Chapman and Ernie Rogers begin to make regular appearances. In 1951 Stevenage became founder members of the Delphian League. V Folbigg can be seen in *Fig 62*; Vic's brother Dereck (Dee) Folbigg played as goalkeeper in 1953 and also for a Delphian League team that toured the Channel Islands and Europe. By then 26, he had had trials for Chelsea and Spurs. In the Autumn of 1951, Stevenage had to play Willesden, Leatherhead, Woodford Town and Hatfield Town in the Herts Charity Shield. Honours won between 1919 and 1951 were shown on page 25 of the Souvenir Programme (*see Fig 65*).

One curiosity has surfaced from the past when a Town centre forward played football with an elephant – not on this occasion a Hitchin Town

If I were a Blackbird ...

Fig 63 – The Stripes in 1950 soon after promotion to the Premier Division of the Spartan League.
Back row, left to right : Bert Smith (Team coach), Brian Scanlon (Manager), A Jackson, Ivan Watson, K Hunt, J Caldecote, Les Taylor, Percy Atkins (Trainer); centre : Dennis (Lummy) Taylor, W Bell, B Johnson (Captain), A Bloxham, Ron Bracey; front : S Lawrence, B Hudson (?) (Photo courtesy D Taylor).

Fig 64 – The Stripes after beating Cheshunt in the FA Cup around 1950.
Back row, left to right : D Hawkins, G Dixon, K Hunt, E Fisher; centre : E Rogers, A Jackson, A Bloxham; front : D Taylor, F Wingate, D Brock, J Chapman, G Hussey.

▼▼▼▼▼▼▼▼▼▼▼▼▼▼▼▼▼▼▼▼▼▼▼▼▼▼

STEVENAGE TOWN FOOTBALL CLUB

Honours between 1919 and 1951

1919-20—Winners, Letchworth Hospital Charity Cup.
1919-20—Champions, North Herts League (Division II).
1919-20—Winners, North Herts Junior (Greg) Cup.
1920-21—Champions, North Herts League (Division II).
1920-21—Winners, Hitchin Hospital Charity Cup.
1921-22—Winners, Hitchin Hospital Charity Cup.
1922-23—Winners, Hitchin Hospital Charity Cup.
1922-23—Champions, North Herts League (Division I).
1922-23—Winners, North Herts Junior Charity Shield.
1923-24—Runners-up, North Herts League (Division I).
1924-25—Finalists, Herts Charity Shield.
1924-25—Winners, Stevenage Nursing Cup.
1925-26—Winners, Stevenage Nursing Cup.
1925-26—Finalists, Hitchin Hospital Cup.
1928-29—Finalists, Stevenage Nursing Cup.
1929-30—Winners, Stevenage Nursing Cup.
1929-30—Finalists, Hitchin Hospital Charity Cup.
1930-31—Champions, South Midlands League (Division II).
1931-32—Champions, North Herts League (Division I).
1931-32—Winners, Stevenage Nursing Cup.
1932-33—Winners, Stevenage Nursing Cup.
1932-33—Winners, North Herts Junior Charity Shield.
1932-33—Winners, Letchworth Hospital Charity Cup.
1932-33—Winners, Herts Charity Shield.
1933-34—Runners-up, Spartan League (Division II).
1933-34—Winners, Letchworth Hospital Charity Cup.
1933-34—Winners, Stevenage Nursing Cup.
1934-35—Runners-up, Spartan League (Division II).
1934-35—Winners, Hitchin Hospital Charity Cup.
1934-35—Winners, Letchworth Hospital Charity Cup.
1935-36—Joint Holders, Hitchin Hospital Charity Cup.
1936-37—Winners, Stevenage Nursing Cup.
1937-38—Runners-up, Spartan League (Division II).
1944-45—Winners, Stevenage Nursing Cup ⎫ Under name of
1945-46—Winners, Stevenage Nursing Cup ⎭ "Stevenage"
1947-48—Runners-up, Spartan League (Division I Eastern).
1947-48—Joint Holders, Knebworth Nursing Cup.
1948-49—Champions, Spartan League (Division I Eastern).
1950-51—Runners-up, Spartan League (Division I Eastern).
1950-51—Joint Holders, Herts Charity Shield.
1950-51—Divisional Finalists, Amateur Cup.

▲▲▲▲▲▲▲▲▲▲▲▲▲▲▲▲▲▲▲▲▲▲▲▲▲▲

Fig 65 – The Honours List 1951 (courtesy V Folbigg)

stopper centre half, but a four-legged member of 'Sanger's Mammoth Circus'. This animal, not a mammoth either, was proclaimed by his trainer to be 'a thorough sportsman, who would not take any mean advantage by striking a man with his trunk'. The striker in question was Bert Leggatt, centre forward for Stevenage in 192–(?) Bert was 5ft 4 inches tall and weighed 10 stone. Despite giving away so much weight, he is on record as saying: 'I felt perfectly safe. We just took alternate shots at goal, and the one who scored most would win a cup, though for the life of me I couldn't imagine what the elephant would do with it if he won it.' Whether the elephant heard the remark or not is unrecorded. Certainly, his degree of motivation was questionable, because Bert won the cup and kept it on top of his piano for the rest of his life.

FA Amateur Cup

There followed years of mixed success in the Delphian League in which the club stayed until 1963, the highest placing being fifth in 1952–3. However, Stevenage Town's reputation as an amateur side to be reckoned with blossomed suddenly in the early fifties. In 1953–4, the club reached the 1st Round proper of the FA Amateur Cup for the first time, eventually losing at home to Wimbledon (3–1) on 19 December 1953. Reports of these matches were filed, often straight after the game, to the offices of the local press. They appeared in the *Hertfordshire Express* or in the *Herts Pictorial* over the pen names of 'The Don' (Don Hills), 'Bird's Eye' (Don Birdsey) or, under a name suggestive of a beer-soaked evening, 'Soccerates' (Ted Long).

The furthest Stevenage had reached in the FA Amateur Cup in previous seasons had been the Divisional Finals – 3rd Qualifying Round – in 1952–53, when they were knocked out by Vauxhall Motors, and three years before that when they were beaten by Letchworth. In 1953 it took them seven matches, including one replay, to reach the 1st Round proper. After beating Spartan League neighbours Letchworth, 4–3 at home on 5 September, they defeated Berkhamsted 3–1 away. The next round was against Potton when Stevenage on their own ground 'just scraped home against the South Midlands League team, 4–3'. Stevenage scored through Dennis Brock who was put through by Johnny Chapman. Lummy Taylor scored before half-time, but then 'Potton bagged two goals before Arthur Bloxham headed home a Taylor centre'. Taylor was Stevenage's star and 'had probably his best game of the season.' He scored again to put Stevenage into the next round.

At Wootton, three weeks later, they outclassed Blue Cross to win 5–3. At Shefford the next week the 'speed and thrust of the young home side probably surprised Stevenage.' Fortunately, Stevenage reserve full-backs

The Town Football Club

Fig 66 – The Stripes in 1952.
Back row, left to right : R Snell (trainer), D Roberts, E Hornett, H Topping, J Mills, M Anthony, C Jennings (team manager); front : A Jackson, D Taylor, C Brennan, C Booty, A Bradbury. (Courtesy The Comet*)*

Mervyn Anthony and 'Taffy' Evans 'had their best games yet for the club' and together with Alan Jackson 'kept a tight rein on Shefford's danger men, Stoten and Johnson'. Nevertheless, Shefford led after eight minutes until Johnny Chapman 'weaved his way through the home defence to score with a perfectly-placed shot. Throughout Chapman was the shining star of the Stevenage firmament' and 'seemed to revel in the difficult conditions'. In the second half, Lummy Taylor 'went close with several goal efforts' to give a 1–1 draw. The following week 'a crowd of about 1000 saw Stevenage make club history by advancing into the 4th qualifying round with a convincing 5–0 win in the replay.' The Stripes 'had the game well won by half-time playing a brand of football to which Shefford just had no answer'. Brock scored from a Taylor centre, Wingate scored from an acute angle and then Brock scored again. 'It was the sort of football that gave Stevenage so many convincing wins last season. Second-half goals came from Rogers and Taylor. Man of the match was unquestionably Taffy Rogers. Here, there and everywhere, Rogers worked like a terrier, and had a hand in more than one of the goals.'

In the Fourth Qualifying round away to Enfield, Stevenage's 'fighting spirit led to triumph' against the Athenian League team by the odd goal in five. The last five minutes saw 'hectic tussles in the Stevenage goalmouth'. Enfield took the lead in 21 minutes, 'after Taylor had seen one of his "specials" kicked off the goal line. The second-half had a sensational start. Within 5 minutes Rogers equalised with a drive from 20 yards, and two minutes later Taylor put the Town in front with a shot that Wood got to, but could only help into the net.' Penalties from both teams concluded the scoring, Alan Jackson shooting home for Stevenage. 'Undoubtedly, one of Stevenage's best displays. Ken Hunt has played few better games, and Mervyn Anthony and Taffy Evans prove such capable substitutes that it is difficult to see how Hawkins and Fisher can regain their places. Man of the match was again Taffy Rogers, who gave Enfield a most harassing afternoon' before a crowd of 1600.

During this cup run, the leading scorer for Stevenage was the speedy, sharp-shooting outside-right, Lummy Taylor with six goals; Wingate, Brock and Jackson each scored three goals, Jackson's all being penalties; other goal scorers were Hussey, Rogers, Chapman and Bloxham. Injuries to a number of senior players, including the right-back Doug Hawkins and the left-back and captain Eric Fisher, resulted in Stevenage fielding 18 different men before November was out. The Club Committee, anticipating a crowd of up to 3000 for the game against Wimbledon, considered ground improvements and obtained estimates for the erection of extra stands and terraces. Admission was to remain at one shilling for adults and eight pence for schoolboys and old age pensioners. The price of admission to the grandstand – by ticket only – was to be two shillings and six pence and to the Supporters' Club stand one shilling.

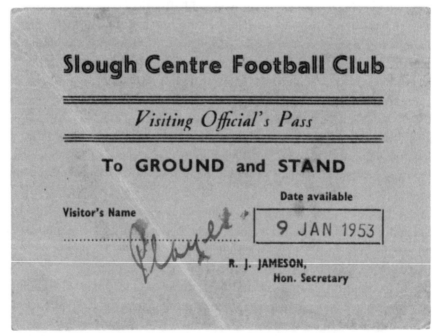

Fig 67 – Lummy Taylor's Player's Pass (courtesy D Taylor)

The *Herts Express* (27 November 1953) felt obliged to add a human, or rather a canine, note to enliven their column. Mr G Leonard Hearne, the club President, had a West Highland Terrier called 'Pip' which came with him to every match. According to the *Express*, the dog is the Club's mascot and wears a large red and white favour on his collar and a smile on his face. Pip sits at his master's feet, wagging his tail, seeming to follow the play with interest. Should Stevenage find themselves at the wrong end of the score at half-time, Pip will be taken to the Stripes' dressing room so that all the players can pat him on the head again before renewing the battle.

Against Wimbledon, Stevenage 'went down with flying colours ... went down fighting after a ding-dong struggle in which they refused to give up hope.' But the Isthmian League team showed more experience than Stevenage and their 'fast and strong forwards gave the Town defence a busy afternoon.' The Stevenage wing-halves had constantly to aid in defence and so 'had less opportunity than usual to give their forwards support, and this was reflected in the fact that the inside men Wingate and Chapman could rarely escape the toils of Munday and Woods.' Prospects were not improved by an eye injury to Dennis Brock. He was substituted before the end. Wimbledon scored first through Cammell before Stevenage drew level through a Wimbledon own goal. Wimbledon regained the lead through a headed goal by Jack Wallis and scored again through Cammell. Jack Wallis – unrelated to the author – was one of two Wallises in the Wimbledon team. 'For Stevenage, Ken Hunt gave a valiant display and Mervyn Anthony had one of his best games. Rogers and Jackson were both tireless.' The attendance was a disappointing 1184.

Stevenage: K Hunt, M Anthony, A Evans, E Rogers, A Jackson, A Bloxham, D Taylor, F Wingate, D Brock, J Chapman, W Hussey.

GAME WITH CORINTHIAN CASUALS

The following year brought a surprise 3–1 home victory against mighty Corinthian Casuals. The Casuals played in chocolate and pink; in the team were several Oxbridge Blues and three amateur internationals. The skipper was Doug Insole, famous as a cricketer, who had also captained Cambridge University at soccer. The match programme describes him as 'an expert at corner taking and frequently makes as extra long throw-in to put opponents' goal in jeopardy.' He played on the right wing. Like several other members of the team, Doug Insole had previously played for Pegasus. Ralph Cowan (right back), Reg Vowels (centre half) and John Dutchman (centre forward) were ex-Pegasus players; Pohn Ahm in goal was a Danish Amateur international and Ralph Cowan, Guy Shuttleworth (right half-back) and John Dutchman were English Amateur

If I were a Blackbird ...

Fig 68 – Mr W Keech, Chairman of Stevenage Town Supporters' Club, presents a clock to Alan Jackson to mark his one hundredth consecutive appearance for the Town. In the background, from left to right, are : E Rogers, D Brock, E Hornett, L Bunyan, J Mills, W Hussey, H Hope, J Chapman, M Anthony. (Courtesy of D Taylor)

internationals. In 1954, Casuals were having a somewhat indifferent season in the Isthmian League. Their glory days had been before the war. They were formed by the amalgamation of Casuals (Amateur Cup winners in 1936) and the renowned Corinthians.

Stevenage Town were captained by Johnny Chapman (No 10, inside left), a lanky but elegant player, and had stalwarts of many seasons in Alan Jackson (right back, Stripes' longest-serving player), Lummy Taylor (right wing), Den Brock (centre forward), Taffy Rogers (right half) and Mervyn Anthony (left back). Alan Jackson can be seen receiving a clock to mark his one hundredth appearance for the club. The Stripes Team Manager assured supporters that his 'boys are just longing for the kick-off whistle to blow. During the last week they have trained harder than ever before ...' Stevenage had brought in an experienced goalkeeper in Ernie Hornett and 'three youngsters well under the age of twenty-one, whom we know will be among the "stars" of the future in Johnny Brett (centre half), Curly Pateman (left half-back) and Jimmy McLafferty (left wing).' As 'The Don' put it: 'The Dismal Jimmies who forecast a six-goal defeat for Stevenage ... backed the wrong horse, but at least they had their money's-worth in witnessing the shock result of the round.'

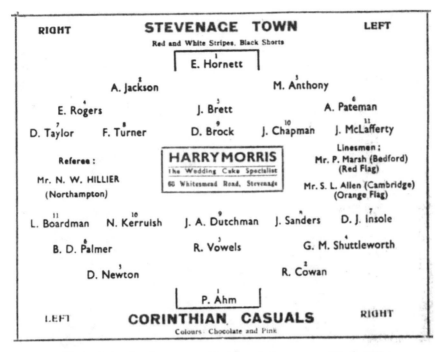

Fig 69 – Team sheets for the game with Casuals (courtesy of Don Hills)

The Town made club history by advancing to the second round for the first time in their history. However, 'in the opening minutes a shock result looked anything but likely. It was not until Casuals took the lead in the 15th minute through Kerruish that the Town came to life – fought back – and equalised just before half-time.' Danny Turner scored from 'a good pass by Taylor after a perfectly-placed goal kick by Hornett.' 'The Don' reckoned Stevenage 'moved into position better, were quicker on the ball, and took their chances splendidly'. Never have I seen the "Stripes" so fit. They set a fast pace for the whole ninety minutes. It was the Casuals who failed to last ... and, at the end, were a well-beaten side.' Ten minutes into the second half, Turner was tripped in the penalty area and 'Taylor made no mistake from the spot.' Eight minutes later Jimmy McLafferty 'drove the final nail in Casuals' coffin with a finely-headed goal from a cross by Rogers.' Hard tackling and keen marking played a big part in the victory. There were 'excellent displays from Jackson and Anthony, Hornett was again in great form and the mastery Rogers gained over John Dutchman was an important factor. Brett, too, played splendidly after a shaky start. Young Curly Pateman was outstanding in this big test. The Casuals' passing, ball-control and approach work generally was pretty to watch, but in front of goal over-eagerness or desperation made them strangely impotent. They usually made one pass too many, which gave the Stevenage defence time to get into position.'

Fig 70 – Mervyn Anthony and goal-keeper Ernie Hornett make sure their boots are well studded on the eve of the game with Pegasus (courtesy D Taylor)

STEVENAGE VERSUS PEGASUS

For the game against Pegasus in the next round on 22 January 1955 the Programme price was increased from threepence to sixpence. Alan Jackson was making his 140th consecutive appearance for the club in twelve successive seasons. The team manager claimed that they 'could hardly have had a more attractive fixture than against Corinthian Casuals' but now 'an even larger plum came out of the hat'. He could 'welcome to London Road many famous names in the world of amateur soccer. It is easily the most glamorous fixture of our long career.' Only one change was made to the team that defeated Casuals; a young Robin Staff replaced McLafferty on the left-wing. Snowy Pateman (left half-back), who had been called up for National Service the previous Thursday, was given permission to play. Peter Taylor in the Match Programme wrote 'our boys will live up to their nickname "The Tigers". We have no stars at Stevenage, but we do have a great team spirit. So let the whistle blow for a good hard sporting game – and please, Cyril Armitage, guard that

STEVENAGE TOWN
FOOTBALL CLUB

(LONDON ROAD, STEVENAGE   PHONE 796)

." THE STRIPES "

FOUNDED 1884

ASSOCIATE MEMBERS OF THE FOOTBALL ASSOCIATION
AND THE HERTS COUNTY LEAGUE; AFFILIATED TO THE
HERTS COUNTY FOOTBALL ASSOCIATION; MEMBERS
OF THE DELPHIAN LEAGUE AND THE NORTH HERTS LEAGUE

PRESIDENT :
G. L. HEARN, ESQ.

OFFICIALS :

Chairman : E. BOSLEY   *Vice-Chairman* : E. J. WALKER
Hon. Secretary : R. G. M. GAME, 138, Letchmore Road, Stevenage
Hon. Treasurer : F. PRESTON, 17 Julians Road, Stevenage
Hon. Team Secretary : C. BOSLEY, 74 Haycroft Road, Stevenage
Hon. Membership Secretary : R. G. PARKER, 115 Sish Lane, Stevenage
Hon. Press Secretary : DON HILLS, 18 Bridge Road, Stevenage

F.A. Amateur Cup   **Saturday, Jan. 22nd, 1955**
(Second Round Proper)   **Kick-off 2.30 p.m.**

STEVENAGE TOWN
versus
PEGASUS

OFFICIAL SOUVENIR PROGRAMME—PRICE SIXPENCE

Lucky NO. 1443

Fig 71 – Official Programme (courtesy of Don Hills)

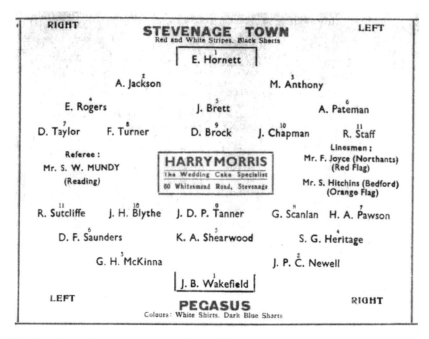

Fig 72 – Team sheets (courtesy of Don Hills)

Blackbird record well.' Town President, G L Hearne, said his chief anxiety was the weather – we have endeavoured to cope with the wetness of the ground putting down ashes to give a better standing. Pegasus can feel, in meeting Stevenage, 'that they are meeting an amateur team where there is no nonsense about secret payments of any description.' The Assistant Team Manager, Eric Fisher, previously a stalwart full-back for Stevenage for many seasons was acknowledged as the 'man behind the scenes'.

The match programme calls Pegasus a 'much more together team than Corinthians Casuals with a defence which is both strong and powerful in physique and difficult to beat. They have a greater strength, too, at half-back and a near perfect blend of cleverness and punch in attack'. The Pegasus side included five amateur internationals and five of the side which had won the Amateur Cup in 1953, when they beat Harwich and Parkeston by six goals to nil. They had also won the cup in 1951 defeating Bishop Auckland. The team included J B Wakefield in goal, an Oxford Blue previously with Northern Nomads; J B C Newell at right-back, a Cambridge Blue; at left-back G H McKinna, an RAF officer and Amateur International, formerly captain of soccer at Oxford and a cricket Blue; S G Heritage at right-half, having switched from inside forward, Oxford soccer captain in 1950; K Shearwood, centre-half, a teacher at Lancing College; Don Saunders, left-half, Amateur International and teacher at Malvern College; A H (Tony) Pawson, Amateur International who had played for Pegasus since their foundation and in the cup finals of 1951 and 1953. He had previously played for Charlton Athletic and captained Oxford at cricket as well as playing for Kent. He was later to be a sports correspondent for *The Observer*. The programme has it 'Still one of the cleverest and most dangerous wing forwards in amateur soccer'. Inside right, G Scanlan, was also a Cambridge Blue; centre forward, J D P Tanner had also played for Pegasus since their formation and was an Amateur International; J H Blythe at inside left was an Oxford Blue working on a PhD in radio-astronomy at Cambridge; finally, on the left wing was Roy Sutcliffe, an Amateur International who had scored two goals in the 1953 Cup Final. The team manager was Joe Mercer, a legendary ex-Arsenal player.

Stevenage had been provided with a dossier on their opponents' strengths and weaknesses, individual characteristics and tactical manoeuvres, by fellow Delphian Leaguers, Dagenham. Since the Delphian League was formed no club had got so far in the Amateur Cup as Stevenage had done in 1954-55. Dagenham hoped to see the 'Stripes' succeed, partly because Pegasus had knocked them out in the previous round, 4–0.

'Pegasus made to fight all the way! Beaten, but not disgraced', wrote 'The Don'. 'Playing before a record crowd on a heavy, fog-shrouded ground, Stevenage in a thrilling and hectic match gave a good account of themselves, and were unfortunate to lose by a 5–2 margin. They had the worst of the "breaks" which occur in any cup-tie.' There was a penalty claim for 'hands' by Shearwood in the first half, when Stevenage were fighting hard to nullify Tanner's breakaway goal in the 27th minute. The centre-forward had received the ball direct from goalie Wakefield, pushed it past Brett and Jackson and raced through to score. For Stevenage, Staff had a shot cleared off the line and, with Wakefield beaten, shot against the cross bar. And so, by half time, Stevenage were a goal down, even though 'Pegasus were still struggling to find their rhythm against a determined and quick-tackling home side.'

'The real turning point came early in the second half.' Immediately after Brock had equalised from Taylor's high centre which the Pegasus goalie failed to hold, Tanner regained the lead for Pegasus from Blythe's angled pass. Stevenage 'fought back with élan and twice Staff went near to levelling the scores.' But Pegasus showed their ability to be quick and dangerous. Within the space of seven minutes they scored three more goals. 'Pawson completed a brilliant solo run by beating Hornett with a grand shot from close in. Scanlan then converted a centre from Sutcliffe in the 71st minute and finally, Blythe scored from another centre from the left-winger' in the 76th minute. The excitement was not over, for Pegasus

If I were a Blackbird ...

PROUD PEGASUS !

In 1953, for the second time in three years, Pegasus carried off the Amateur Cup, beating Harwich and Parkeston by the unequalled score of 6–0. Pictured in the moment of triumph is their captain, Don Saunders, holding aloft the trophy as he had done previously in 1951 when Pegasus beat Bishop Auckland 2–1 in another memorable Wembley final.

TONY PAWSON

GORDON MCKINNA

Fig 73 – Proud Pegasus as pictured in the Official Programme. Above, Don Saunders (Captain) (courtesy of Don Hills).

'were awarded a doubtful penalty as a result of Tanner tripping over Anthony's legs. Hornett pushed out Saunder's spot-kick and dived on the ball before the left-half could crack the rebound into the net. The incident put new life into Stevenage, and immediately afterwards Brock scored their second goal. The "Stripes" were still attacking when the final whistle blew.'

'The Don' summed up: 'Although the home defence gave a creditable display considering the calibre of the opposition, they never really found an answer to those amateur international wingers, Pawson and Sutcliffe, while Tanner, Blythe and Scanlan remained a constant menace in the middle.' Joe Mercer thought Stevenage had put up a fine fight. 'I was very worried for a few minutes early in the second half', he said.

Fig 74 – The Town 1931–32 in front of the grandstand. One spectator sports a Stripes scarf (courtesy of Clive Abrey)

THE TOWN GROUND

The tiny town ground was just off the London Road, and opposite Geo King's Factory on the other side of the railway. Bleakly inhospitable, mostly grass and cinders with scarcely any shelter, with 'stands' such as were very appropriate for the 'spartan league'. There was no turnstile. You entered the ground at the gate, tendering your money at the hatch of a small shed. The pitch was surrounded by a metal rail but, apart from some cinders, behind this and in front of it was grass. On the West side was a crude shelter made of corrugated iron which restrained a proportion of the elements. This structure faced the 'grandstand' at the back of which lay the changing rooms. The grandstand of ancient creosoted timbers held when full perhaps a hundred spectators in four to five tiers.

In post-war years, new playing kit was expensive and war veterans returned from more hazardous tournaments wore their own faded shorts of varying lengths. The 'Stripes' defined them, and the slight shabbiness was a token of proper and pure amateur status, to be contrasted with the silky sheen of the yellow and black kit of our snooty neighbours, semi-professional Hitchin Town. We had occasionally to play Hitchin in cup matches and the result was always a heated local derby with considerable mutual ill-will. These occasions would see a steady stream of people moving towards the ground, even a special constable or two to maintain a scarcely disturbed decorum. At the end of the game a little congestion near the exit gate might lead to short delays, but trouble in the crowd was unheard of! How different from the First Division matches my dad would take me to in London to watch the aristocrats of the game, especially the Spurs at White Hart Lane and the Gunners at Highbury. Here you jockeyed for a standing position on the terraces with a not too dismal view, you sought out a little breathing space so as to avoid the frightening surges in the crowd and the oppressive scrum pressing you into the barricades.

One exciting encounter with Hitchin Town was in the Second Qualifying Round of the FA Cup in the 'fifties' . The game on 11 October was abandoned after 38 minutes because of torrential rain; Stevenage had given one of their best performances of the season. Tony Cooper, the Stevenage skipper, had 'taken a gamble by electing to kick against the driving rain.' Lummy Taylor, on the right wing, 'was particularly dangerous, and early on Gibbs did well to head away a Taylor centre.' Lummy 'flashed into the picture again with a hard shot which Edwards saved close to the upright.' But 'with their halves and fullbacks swarming upfield,' Hitchin had opportunites on the break. On one of these, 'Guile capped Hills' cleverness by smartly steering the ball wide of Hornett to put Hitchin ahead in the 32nd minute. Three minutes later, the biggest cheer of the afternoon greeted Stevenage's equaliser. Lusty lost possession, and Taylor broke through to score with a magnificent cross-shot.' The replay, on the following Wednesday, will 'always be remembered by Stevenage supporters as 'The game we should have won'. Playing progressive football, the Stripes led 2–0 and 3–1 in the first half, and a quarter-of-an-hour from the end were still holding grimly to their 3–2 half-time lead.' At the final whistle, 'superior fitness rather than superior football' saw Hitchin through.

Taylor took a free-kick which was headed wide of the Hitchin goalie by Tufnell for Stevenage's first goal. Fourteen minutes later Tufnell

Fig 75 – Quick to take advantage. Neville Overman scores with, left to right, John Lusty, John French, Lummy Taylor and goalie Peter Edwards (courtesy of D Taylor)

centred with the Hitchin defence in a tangle and Neville Overman, the Stevenage centre forward, 'wriggled clear of the melee to score at close range.' (Fig 75) The next five minutes saw penalties for both sides, Bradbury converting for Stevenage. In the second half, 'Hitchin piled on the pressure against a tiring defence' and first Figg scored after bursting through before Hammond completed the scoring to give Hitchin a 4–3 win. Stevenage replied with 'a grandstand finish with shots by Tufnell and Draper which narrowly missed the target.'

Stevenage: E Hornett, R Morton, A Cooper, M Ward, A Jackson, A Bradley, D Taylor, P Kies, N Overman, J Draper, W Tufnell.

Fig 76 – Worthy of their Stripes. The team that mounted a fighting display in the replayed cup-tie against Hitchin.
Back row, left to right : Len Bayliss (trainer-coach), Mick Ward, Alan Jackson, Harry Morton, Ernie Hornett, Tony Cooper, Arthur Bradbury, ? Chapman (assistant to Len Bayliss); front : Lummy Taylor, Paul Kies, Neville Overman, Jim Draper, Bill Tufnell (courtesy of D Taylor)

Stevenage and Hitchin clashed quite regularly in the Herts Senior Cup. The first game in 1952 resulted in a 1–1 draw. In the replay at Stevenage on 6 December 1952, the Stripes secured a resounding 4–1 victory. 'Stevenage were worthy winners. Hitchin failed because they kept the ball too close and tried to dribble past the opposition,' opined 'Bird's Eye'. The rival paper had 'Hitchin "lost" in the snow: Straight-for-goal Stevenage.' 'Hitchin's failure to adapt themselves to a slippery, snow-covered pitch brought about their defeat by a lively, robust Stevenage team'. Centre-forward Lummy Taylor was in great form, and 'at the end was chaired off the field by jubilant Stevenage supporters. He had ploughed his way through the snow – and the Hitchin defence – to score three first-class goals. Hitchin's more attractive style of football proved ineffective against the quick, hard-tackling Stevenage defenders, who seemed to revel in the snow.' Initially, 'swinging the ball from wing to wing, Hitchin swept to the offensive. Poor finishing, and several smart saves from Folbigg' kept Hitchin out. Stevenage half-backs Alan Jackson and Arthur Bloxham 'really proved their worth. Jackson did the work of two men, keeping Brian Smith subdued and helping the rather shaky Ross to keep Alec Smith in check.' From a Bloxham pass, 'Taylor produced a burst of speed to round Jack Fisher before beating Hogg with a hard, low shot.' Although Hitchin quickly equalised, Taylor scored again before half-time. Two goals by Stevenage in the first 10 minutes of the second half 'clinched the result.' A fumble by the Hitchin goalie produced a goal for Chapman and he had a 'hand in the final goal, putting the ball through to Taylor to beat all others in the race for goal.' Stevenage inside forwards Johnny Chapman and Frank Wingate 'had an impressive match; the pair did a great deal of work both in defence and attack.' According to 'Bird's Eye', it was a 'dispirited Hitchin that trooped off the field ... but Stevenage's win was no fluke.'

Stevenage: D Folbigg, D Hawkins, E Fisher, G Ross, A Jackson, A Bloxham, T Daly, F Wingate, D Taylor, J Chapman, F Pateman.

Stevenage and Hitchin met again in the Herts Senior Cup around 1954 or so. Stevenage caught Hitchin on the rebound from a strenuous game against Millwall and won 3–1 at home. 'Bird's Eye', under the headline, 'Stevenage shock a so very lifeless Hitchin,' reckoned that 'Hitchin certainly played as though they had a hangover from the intoxications of the clashes with the "Lions". Stevenage, however, gave a very determined display.' In their first real attack, after 12 minutes, Taylor took a free-kick for 'hand-ball' and played a ball across goal from which Neville Overman headed home. Three minutes later, 'Taylor scored a second for the "Stripes" and I fancy that second goal was the real turning-point in the game'. Taylor, still a live-wire even if he must now be classed as a veteran, made it 3–0 just before half-time and probably put paid to any lingering hopes Hitchin may have had of saving the day.' Peter Hammond did get a goal back from a penalty but Stevenage 'were always the more dangerous'. Billy Tufnell and Jimmy Draper went close to increasing the lead.'

Stevenage: E Hornett, D McKay, A Cooper, M Ward, A Jackson, R Bell, D Taylor, P Kies*, N Overman, J Draper, W Tufnell.

In 1953, another Herts Senior Cup 'Derby' was played at Hitchin on 28 November. For Stevenage, Eric Fisher returned for them after an injury to left-back Evans. 'Bird's Eye' reported 'Hitchin scramble to victory' and even though 'the standard of football' was disappointingly low, the 3085 spectators could find some consolation in that thrills were plentiful enough.' The game was 'hard, fast and exciting but with the finer points largely forgotten,' Hitchin winning in the end 2–1. Hitchin had led from the 16th minute from a headed goal by Ward, 'but when Frank Wingate slammed home an equaliser with only 14 minutes to go, Stevenage hopes went soaring. But within two minutes, the Hitchin left-wing Kitchener moved to the centre, took a pass from John Ward and gave Ken Hunt no chance with a perfectly-placed, winning shot.' Generally defences were on top but both sides made chances. 'Stevenage were better on the right-wing than on the left, for Taylor, even if he has lost some of his speed, was frequently dangerous, and Wingate worked tremendously hard'. The right-wing pair had the advantage of having Taffy Rogers behind them, and the ebullient Welshman was as good as any player on the field. A large bouquet, too, for Alan Jackson, who can have few superiors in the county as a centre-half in the stopper mold, while Mervyn Anthony had no reason to be dissatisfied with a display against the formidable Kitchener.' The Stevenage line was led by 'the dashing Brock'. This was Dennis Brock who had been recruited from Hertford. A strong, direct and forcible player, he had made an auspicious debut in a game against the Delphian League leaders, Dagenham, which Stevenage won 5–2 away from home. However, in the game against Hitchin, Jack Fisher ensured that he 'had little chance to shine.'

Stevenage: K Hunt, M Anthony, E Fisher, E Rogers, A Jackson, A Bloxham, D Taylor, F Wingate, D Brock, J Chapman, W Hussey.

My old friend Mike Palmer was apprentice reporter for the Pictorial and used to write match reports for Don Hills at the rate of a half-penny a line. Don Birdsey (Bird's Eye) regularly changed all his soccer filings; so ardently committed a Hitchin Town fan was he that he forbade Mike to report on Hitchin–Stevenage games. For the Pegasus game Mike was asked to phone the copy in to the *Evening News*. As there was no phone

* Paul (originally Pal) Kies was a Hungarian refugee

available to the press at the ground, he was obliged to cycle to the High Street and use the phone outside his grandfather's old cycle shop.

THE END OF THE TOWN GROUND

Around 1960, Stevenage Town FC was informed that the land on which their ground stood was wanted by the Development Corporation for the Civic Centre development and the new railway station. The Development Corporation's proposed site for the new ground was on part of the old Stevenage sewage works, the Corporation hinting that they might eventually build a modern sports stadium there, a dream never realised. By the late fifties the New Town was growing rapidly and had formed its own football club, Stevenage Rangers. Based on the premise that one big club would be better than two small ones, Stevenage Rangers and Stevenage Town amalgamated at the close of the 1955–6 season, under the name Stevenage FC. In 1960 'Town' was returned to the club's title and in 1963 turned semi-professional and joined the Southern League. After some years of moderate success, financial problems overcame the club, which disbanded in 1968. A new club, Stevenage Athletic, was formed the same year. By 1970–1 this club had been elected to the Southern League where fortunes were mixed, their best season being 1973–4 when they came seventh. The club's final season in 1975–6 promised much with the old Spurs player, Alan Gilzean, as manager, but they ended that season at the bottom of the table. Financial problems led to their resignation from the Southern League. Stevenage FC was formed (or re-formed) in 1976, first of all playing at King George V Playing Fields until the Broadhall Way ground was refurbished in 1980. Stevenage then added 'Borough' to their title.

Perhaps, if you were to linger a while on the asphalt of the Civic Centre and listen hard enough, you might catch an echo of the Blackbird song or catch a fleeting glimpse of Lummy shimmying down the wing again while Alan Jackson holds the centre firm.

10

THE GRAMMAR SCHOOL

THE MEMORIAL GATES

For some years I would dream I was wearing my Grammar School cap, though no longer a schoolboy nor standing anywhere near the School. There is a compulsion to keep it on. At other times I sense the distinct absence of my cap and a necessity to be wearing it; somehow I have left it behind. It was a rule of the school that caps should be worn in the town by all pupils except Sixth formers; caps should be removed when entering the school through the Memorial Gates.

Fig 77 – The Memorial Gates in 1930 looking into the school grounds. On the right, is the creeper-covered headmaster's house. In the distance, to the left of the tree, can be seen the frontage of the pre-war school hall with a notice-board to the left of the main doors. On the far left, the gothic window is set in the west-end of the science laboratory. (Drawing from a photograph courtesy Richard Stephens)

After the First World War the Old Boys' Association began to raise money for a memorial to old pupils killed in the war, but the fund and the first Association foundered in 1924. Two years later fund-raising began again and Trinity College, Cambridge, which has a long association with the school, promised to match funds raised locally to facilitate a plan for Gates to be made by local craftsmen.

The Gates were designed by G H Russell of Hitchin, the ironwork wrought by C W Roast of Baldock and red brick piers with Portland stone caps were erected by an Old Boy of the school, C J Bond of Stevenage. A stone tablet on the left hand pillar reads:

'These gates were erected by the Old Boys and the Foundation in memory of Alleynians who fell in the Great War, 1914–1918.' A similar tablet on the right-hand pillar bears 15 names. The two shields on the ironwork, carrying the arms of Trinity College and of Thomas Alleyne, were made by F L Slow, one of the masters. The gates were officially opened on school Speech Day, 1930, by the President of the Old Boys' Association, W Hitchcock, with the words:

'May these gates be to all who enter, the symbol of sacrifice, without which no man can attain to manliness or the highest knowledge.'

The Alleynian, in a solemn editorial of 1930, asserted that the 'two most impressive moments in the school life of a boy are the first and the last: when he passes through the Gates for the first time and when he passes out of them for good. The first moment is one of mystery and wonderment. He feels with every step he takes that he is immersing himself more and more in the mystery of the School "ethos" ... Between that entry and this exit should take place the making of a man ... The shadow of those gates should fall upon him as a blessing of rich promise.'

Less respect was shown to the Gates by delivery van drivers in the years after the Second World War. After several incidents when a stone cap had been displaced and a whole pillar demolished more than once, the gateway was widened. Bars were added to each gate where they meet but are not entirely in keeping with the original design.

FOUNDATION OF THE GRAMMAR SCHOOL

The school was founded in 1558 by Thomas Alleyne whose family name was variously spelt Alen, Allen, Alleyne, Alleyen, Allyene, Allyn and Alyn. He was a cousin of the doctrinally nimble-footed Vicar of Bray, Simon Aleyn, to whom he left 'one little white silver cup, with a featherbed bolster and a covering, and also one of my fine surplices.' His will begins 'Thomas Allyn, clerk and parson ...' and leaves money to found schools in Stone and Uttoxeter in Staffordshire and in Stevenage. My sources for much of the historical detail in this chapter are 'An Innings well played. The story of Alleyne's School Stevenage'[26] and '1558-1958. Happy are thy men. The story of Alleyne's Grammar School, Stevenage, Herts.'[27]

Thomas Alleyne may once have been a curate at Shirland in the Lichfield diocese whose Bishop, Geoffrey Blythe, had previously been Master of the King's Hall, Cambridge. This establishment later became part of Henry VIII's foundation of Trinity College. Thomas Alleyne entrusted Trinity College with the future of the school. He was made Rector of Thornhill, near Dewsbury in Yorkshire in 1513 and became Rector of Stevenage some time before 1526, when he is recorded as donating money towards one of Cardinal Wolsey's projects. In Stevenage he lived in Woodfield, Rectory Lane, now a private nursing home. Alleyne liked the proximity of Stevenage to London, which was a comfortable day's ride away. He had several friends and relations there, including his brother Ralph Alleyne, a prosperous grocer and later Alderman and Sheriff of London. His cousin Joan had married John Lesley, a wealthy goldsmith, who later became Lord Mayor of London. In 1547, part of Ralph's estate was left to Thomas Alleyne 'to be used for charitable purposes.' During this period, the furtherance of education as a charitable enterprise had been decreed by Edward VI, a policy continued by both Mary and Elizabeth. Many schools were founded, including the Public Schools of Shrewsbury (1551), Repton (1559) and Rugby (1567). Alleyne is likely to have carefully planned the foundation of the school and discussed it with the more prominent townspeople of Stevenage. He must have ridden to Cambridge to confer with the authorities at Trinity College about the proposed school and the lands and estates whose rents would pay for it. Trinity did very well out of the lands and properties left in its charge. When he died, the income was between £80 and £100 annually, then a large sum; the income from the estates rose faster than the schoolmaster's wages which didn't increase until the Nineteenth Century.

THE FIRST HEADMASTER

Thomas Alleyne also left forty shillings a year for an exhibition for one poor scholar to attend the University of Cambridge. A codicil to the will listed the lands to be put in the care of Trinity and the provision for schools; estates in Leicestershire, Kent, Staffordshire, Hertfordshire and the City of London provided rents 'amounting to the clear yearly value of four score pounds or there about.' The codicil specifically nominates Marcus Daune as the Stevenage schoolmaster. Since Thomas Alleyne took great pains in setting up the school, even specifying the rules that were to be followed by the boys, Daune must already have been a schoolmaster – perhaps running 'Alleyne's School' before 1558.

THOMAS ALLEYNE'S ENTRY IN THE BURIAL REGISTER

An impressive seventeen lines of Latin, dated 3 August 1558, were composed by the Rector William Pratt. It begins, in translation: 'Thomas Alleyne, a most venerable man, formerly Rector of this church and founder of three public schools for boys, for their teaching and training in letters and good living, one at Stevenage in the county of Hertford, the other two ... And to the master and teacher of each school he gave £13.6.8d as annual stipend; and also a charity of £5.6.8d graciously and munificently given to be forever distributed in equal parts, as his final gift, to four poor men of the parish of Stevenage in the county of Hertford in which parish Thomas Alleyne breathed his last.' The will requires the four poor men to pray for his soul; they were to be paid four times a year 'at the feast of the Nativity of St John the Baptist, St Michael the Archangel, the birth of our Lord God and the annunciation of our blessed lady, Saint Mary the Virgin or within 12 days ensuing any of the feasts.'

THE SCHOOL BUILDINGS

Given the highly detailed will, it is odd that no site for the school was specified unless it was the case that a school already existed in Stevenage. It is likely that Daune may have started the Alleyne school at his own house in Stevenage High Street, and probably moved to the Brotherhood House in 1558, also in the High Street. The Brotherhood House had been established by the longstanding Fraternity of the Holy Trinity, a small guild of townsmen concerned with religious brotherhood and observance. This house was bequeathed by Edward Wilshere to the townsmen of Stevenage, who had already established a fund to support a school. There are some very old parts of the Alleyne's School House (rear part of the Headmaster's House) which were probably part of the original Brotherhood House, suggesting it was moved to this new site.

The Wilshere bequest was probably the spur to the building of the Old Schoolroom around 1562. The timber frame utilised beams from the old chapel in the High Street used by the Brotherhood and re-built near the School House on Brotherhood lands. The wooden framing supported a typical vernacular building equally useful as a house, chapel or school.

The school was relatively generously endowed with buildings and land provided by the Brotherhood and money from Alleyne to pay the

Fig 78 – The Old School Room. Drawing from a photograph of the interior from around 1920 (courtesy Richard Stephens). The old school desks survived until the 1950's but by then the plaster casts of the low reliefs by Harry Bates had been moved to the school hall. Above the fireplace can be seen 'Socrates Teaching the People in the Agora' and on the left 'Harvest' and on the right 'Springtime'.

schoolmaster. Subsequent endowments were added to the behests. In 1596 Edward Nodes gave the Bury Mead and later his grandson added to this endowment. However, the master had a double task. Not only was he to run Alleyne's as a 'grammar' school based on the classical education in Latin, he was also required to teach the younger and poorer boys of the town – the 'Pettits' – their elementary work in English. If the master needed help, he must organise and pay for this himself. Most schoolmasters found it necessary to take a curacy in addition or private pupils to supplement their incomes, and this situation persisted for centuries.

THE RULES

Thomas Alleyne wrote, or had written for him, a set of rules to govern all three grammar schools. The original document is kept at Trinity College. One of the first Rules makes clear that boys presenting themselves for education should already be reasonably well educated in English 'having learned the booke of the eight parts of speech in Englishe and very perfectly can say the declensions and can give anie persons in the verbe parte and have afterwards learned the concords of grammar, commonly called the English Rules.' Only then could they be accepted to learn the unremitting Latin at the Grammar School.

'Schollers shall come into the schoole before seaven of the clocke in the morning from Michaelmasse till Our Lady day in Lent; And from Our Ladie Day in Lent until Michaelmasse againe they shall come into the schoole before six of the clocke in the morninge: sub poena virgae – under threat of the rod.' These long hours are quite normal for the 16th and 17th centuries when rising at dawn and retiring to bed soon after dark resulted in the main from lack of safe lighting. Each Rule ended with 'sub poena virgae,' the last reading: 'I will that all my schollers at their first entrance into my schoole shall give two pence apiece to a poor scholler appointed by the master to keepe the school cleane and to provide rods.'

UPHEAVALS IN THE NINETEEN HUNDREDS

A number of vicissitudes beset the school after 1600, including withholding of rents and refusals by the master to teach the Pettits. By the early Nineteenth Century, the school had deteriorated and the authorities at Trinity College recognised this. A highly critical report on the school was prepared by the Charity Commissioners in 1833, reporting that Headmaster Bradbury was now 77, impoverished and exhausted; he was charging 15s a quarter to teach very little to only 5 Scholars. Pettits were still attending the school but their education was rudimentary. Trinity offered the Rector of Stevenage an additional salary of £75 in order to obtain a competent master, bringing the total salary to nearly £120; the parish was required to do any necessary repairs. Subsequently, Trinity appointed the Rev J Osborne Seager M A as Master in 1836.

Criticism from the town was still being voiced. They were disinclined to allow what they saw as their school filling their sons' heads with a dead language and useless information, especially at a cost of 15s a quarter. The greater part of the Trustees preferred a Commercial Education to fit their sons for business or for trade. Wesleyan Methodists had tried to have their sons admitted to Alleyne's. Both Rector and Headmaster Seager refused to countenance this, in consequence of which Dissenters and townspeople joined forces in 1846 to petition Trinity alleging misappropriation of funds by Seager. The next year Seager left Alleyne's when he was presented with the opportunity of setting up his own school. The Swan Inn, just down the High Street from Alleyne's, fell vacant and Seager bought it to open 'The Grange School'. Seager started it off with almost all the pupils from Alleyne's, especially those with richer parents, and advertised it as a 'Preparatory School' for Eton and Harrow. At Alleyne's the replacement master was Robert Ambler.

MILLICE CULPIN'S LETTER

Grandpa's uncle, Millice Culpin, recounted in a 1927 letter from Australia to Headmaster Thorne his recollections of Ambler and of the school in the 1850s. H P Thorne became Headmaster in 1915 and retired in 1945.

Millice Culpin started at Alleyne's when he was 8 years old. 'I went to school under Mr Robert Ambler in January 1854, and I remained until Christmas 1858. I remember Revd J O Seager as the proprietor of a boarding school, conducted in the premises that were the site of the Swan Inn, a grand coaching establishment.

'In my time the school building was a barn-like structure approached by a stile from Bury Mead, with a huge cross-beam above the centre of the hall. When the plaster was cleared off the beam, some very fine carving was revealed.

'One of my sisters was a pupil of Mrs Ambler when I was a student under Mr Ambler. In 1857 and 1858 Mrs Ambler was equal to conducting the school business when illness laid the Master low. All (both girls and boys) were together in the schoolroom.

'In those days a Queen Anne gateway gave accommodation on the north to Bates the Builder, and on the south to B Moules the Baker.'

This letter is the oldest eye-witness description of life at the school that survives.

Millice Culpin's family left Stevenage in 1864 and he took a Medical degree in London before emigrating to Australia. He was the father of

Millais Culpin referred to in Chapter 6. Millice is describing the old schoolroom, still in use in the early 1950s as a classroom. As fifth formers, we listened in its sun-moted air to George Partridge leading us through the beauties of Shakespeare. The Amblers, it would seem, not only ran a kind of co-educational school for a short time – there were no girls left by 1860 – but also provided either a Classical education (15s a quarter) or a Commercial education (7s.6d per quarter). Both types of education were of a low standard and the strain on Ambler seems to have led to long bouts of illness. Complaints and petitions about the inferior buildings and the poor quality of the teaching eventually led to Ambler's resignation.

THE NEW SCHOOLROOM

In 1869 Trinity came up with funds to build a new schoolroom and to enlarge the Master's house. The *Herts Express* of May 1869, reported:

'Within the last three months a new and handsome little building has sprung up under the able hands of Messrs Bates and Warren, near the National Schools and facing the North Road. Trinity College, Cambridge, having provided the necessary funds (about £550) for erecting a new grammar school, more adequate to the wants of the town than the old one, the last finishing touches are being put to the new building, which presents quite an attractive appearance.

'Entering at the Gothic porch on the west end, and passing through the portico, we come into a light well-ventilated appartment, 40 feet long by 17 feet wide, with open timbered roof of stained deal, about 23 feet high, boarded floor, and a solid wainscotting of Portland cement running round the base to a height of about four feet above the ground. This is the chief schoolroom and is intended to accommodate 60 or 70 pupils. Through a folding screen and double-doors we come into the old schoolroom, but so altered and improved that we should hardly recognise it but for its position. The walls have been modernised, the old roof opened up, the panelling restored, and a dreary barn transmogrified into a massive and commodious apartment, 24 feet by 16 feet ... giving space for some 40 scholars. This room is entered by a separate porch at the south eastern extremity. The bell-turret, pointed and handed, rises 25 feet above the crest of the roof, and answers at once the purposes of a bell-cot and a ventilator for both rooms, being placed over the junction of the two.'

Fig 79 – The New Schoolroom aka the Science Lab.
Drawing from a photograph (courtesy Richard Stephens) after refurbishment in 1928. Bottles of chemical reagents can be seen on the shelves to the left and balances for weighing materials are aligned along the benching on the right. Through the door at the far end can be seen the Bates' relief above the Old Schoolroom fireplace.

If I were a Blackbird ...

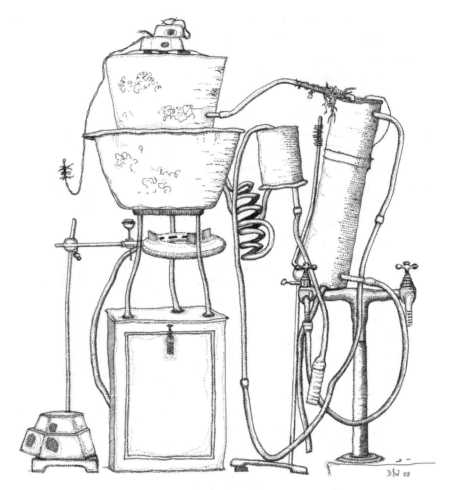

Fig 80 – The Starkey Still aka 'Stillius Starkinorus'
'This remarkable piece of apparatus was invented by Professor Jaroslav
Starkey in the 20th century AD. Using this type of apparatus it is possible to
produce the most impure distilled water ever obtained. It is also ideal for
producing floods in laboratories, or fogs, or sound effects for a witches'
cauldron in Macbeth. The principle of the process, underlying the design of this
machine, is simple, ie by passing water in at one end, and through a maze of
rubber tubing, piping and tin cans, one is bound to get water coming out of the
other end. The apparatus both keeps together and works by faith. Coal gas and
an inefficient water supply are, however, additional factors. When the machine
is in motion, it emits peculiar rumbling sounds, with bubbling and hissing
noises at regular intervals; the weights on top are necessary to subdue the
natural exuberance of the machine while the string and other picturesque
fittings are to satisfy its vanity. The inventor has said about his apparatus that,
by looking at it, one could not possibly dream it could be a still, and
consequently, to date, he has had no trouble with the excise men. Bottles of 'Rye
whiskey', of doubtful quality, can be obtained from the above named professor
for the reasonable sum of half-a-crown.' (Re-drawn from an original by the
author)

STINKS AND BILGE

In my time, the 'new schoolroom' was devoted to 'Stinks and Bilge', becoming the science laboratory. Such practical work as we managed in biology and chemistry was undertaken there, perched on rather uncomfortable stools. Quiet days were spent dissecting the dogfish, the frog and the laboratory rat or sectioning specimens of plants with cut-throat razors. Various pieces of physics apparatus, such as a Whimshurst machine, were demonstrated by Jack Starkey with theatrical aplomb on the bench at the other side of the partition in the old schoolroom. The laboratory was littered with old equipment and jars and bottles full of hazardous chemicals. The science sixth form – two of us, usually – were sometimes tempted towards the frivolous. Spontaneous combustion could be achieved by pouring a small quantity of liquid glycerol into a pile of potassium permanganate crystals. On one occasion, a chunk of solid sodium was hurled into the school pond, where it whirligigged round and round the surface, burning fiercely in a volley of minor explosions.

Just post-war, austerity gravely limited expenditure on equipment and materials. Wasting money on a commercial still for producing distilled water must have been unthinkable to a hands-on do-it-yourselfer like Jack Starkey. Instead, he produced distilled water of his own from an apparatus of which Heath Robinson would have been proud. My drawing of this equipment with legend appended, done in an idle moment, was snaffled by my fellow student and somehow found its way to the Masters' Common Room. I next saw it as a reproduction in the School Magazine under the heading 'Stillius Starkinorus'.

MORE SCHOOL BUILDINGS

The same edition of the *Herts Express* which described this new schoolroom explained the organisation of the school under a new headmaster, G Litting:

'The local trust fund also keeps in repair the master's house, which is large and commodious, and affords ample accommodation for 15 boarders, that being the number to which the master is now restricted ...

'Boys under 11 years of age must pay £3 a year, between 11 and 13 £5 a year, above 13 £6 a year for instruction which includes, besides the ordinary 'English education', elementary mathematics, Latin, French and drawing, with elementary science and vocal music into the bargain if required. Instead of gratuitous education, a scheme has been arranged by which four boys in each grade may win sufficient money prizes to pay their school fees, each exhibition being tenable for two years.' Litting's own interest in science is shown by his support of the local inventor, Nathan Hodgson, who lived in the High Street, somewhere between the

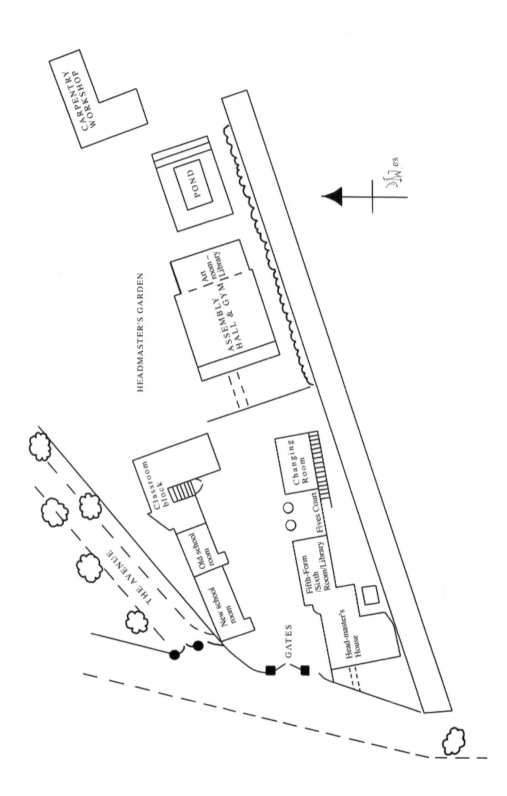

◀ *Fig 81 – Ground plan of the school 1945–1950.*
The Avenue with its own gates lay to the north of the school boundary. Just south of this the new schoolroom and the old schoolroom abutted onto the Classroom Block built in 1905. To the north of the Assembly Hall, Art room and pond the Headmaster's garden was laid out. To the east of the Carpentry Shop, a splendid wooden building, were magnificent lawns and grass tennis courts inherited from the Stevenage Croquet Club and the Carlton Tennis Club, both of which went out of existence in around 1940. South of the school yard and the Memorial Gates were the Headmaster's House adjacent to the Old Library of Fifth/Sixth-Form Room. The Fives Court separated this from the Changing Room. The south boundary was formed by the long shed of the Vincent-HRD works (The Maltings).

Fig 82 – The School buildings, Vincent-HRD works and Grange Preparatory School from the air just before the war.
Far left of the picture are the Memorial Gates with the New Schoolroom behind and the 1905 Classroom block. To the right of the gates is the Headmaster's House and further back the School Hall.
The War Memorial on the Bowling Green is overlooked from the left by the Publix Cinema, and by the large white house, once the Bates' family home and building yard, and then the home of Phil Vincent. The Vincent/HRD showroom doors are behind the tree.
On the right is the Grange Preparatory School, including the elaborate porch added by Seager, using columns from the dismantled gallery in St Nicholas' Church. Further left is the old Swann Inn entrance (the 'Queen Anne archway' mentioned by Millice Culpin) whose white double doors allowed coaches through to the courtyard and the stables beyond. (By kind permission from Stevenage Museum.)

White Hart and the Coach and Horses and invented the 'Little Gem Knife Cleaner'. Litting provided an interest-free loan so that the Cleaner could be patented.

In 1905 the Endowed Schools Act encouraged Trinity to fund a further building programme. The 'Classroom Block' of four classrooms and a large dormitory (later a gymnasium) over a covered playground, subsequently the 'Fives Court', completely altered the appearance of the School yard. More buildings were added in the years 1931–2, long overdue for a school containing 124 pupils. An up-to-date Changing Room was built on the end of the Fives Court, the Gymnasium was converted to a classroom reached by external cast iron stairs and the old Junior Changing Room was altered to provide a Masters' Common Room. When I first attended the school in 1945, the classroom became our Form Room.

An Assembly Hall was erected on part of the Headmaster's garden. This seated 250 and combined the functions of gymnasium and Dining Hall. It had a classroom on a higher level at one end which could be used as a stage. Facing the hall interior were three plaster casts in relief of works by the best known English sculptor in this type of work, Harry Bates ARA. Bates was an old boy of the school and son of Joseph Bates the Builder, who lived between the Headmaster's house and the Grange. The main relief shows 'Socrates Teaching the People in the Agora'; the bronze of which this is the first cast had won Harry Bates the Royal Academy Gold Medal. It is now in Owen's College, Manchester. Socrates is depicted sitting in the market place at Athens eagerly speaking to a number of listening figures, who represent the 'ages of man', from youth to maturity. There were two casts on either side of the Dining Hall stage; the one on the right 'Springtime' and on the left 'Harvest'. Both these panels are in low relief. Their somewhat weather-beaten appearance is the result of standing for many years in the porch of a house at Cory's Mill, before being presented to the school in 1918. The low reliefs were originally hung in the Old Schoolroom. In 1936 the Hall Stage became a Library/Art Room, having previously served as a carpentry workshop. In 1934 an Upper Changing Room had been added above the 1931 Changing

Fig 83 – St Nicholas' School, Bury Mead opened as the Stevenage National School in 1834. The New Rector of Stevenage, Rev Robert Baker, had promoted the erection of the school having agreed with the Stevenage Trustees that the education of their children required urgent attention. It cost £709 – 3s – 11d to build, including the Master's house. Most of the money was contributed by local people. 116 boys and 91 girls enrolled immediately, removing most of the Pettits from Bradbury's tuition at Alleynes. (Drawing from photograph courtesy of Margaret Ashby)

Room and a new Carpentry Workshop was built on the far side of the pond. When new Bicycle Sheds took the place of the temporary sheds constructed by the boys as a Carpentry project, the school was adequately housed for the first time since the First World War. An inspection by the Board of Education in 1934 reported it 'eminently satisfactory'.

SCHOLARSHIP BOYS

Before the Butler Education Act, most boys paid fees as day pupils but a proportion were admitted under the free place scheme. In 1922, for instance, 24 boys on the school roll of 100 pupils had free places. The others were charged £12 per term tuition fees. My Culpin uncles, Ben and John, both attended the school but whether on Free Places or not, I do not know. As young lads, they appear in a photograph of the 3rd Stevenage (Alleyne's Own) Scout Troop for 1916[26].

The Education Act provided free Grammar School education to pupils passing a Scholarship exam – the 'Eleven Plus.' The Act required all County 'recognised' schools such as Alleyne's to undertake a series of costly improvements and developments in return for continued Government maintenance. If the school's endowments allowed this, they became 'grant-aided' schools with the County Council paying half the other costs. The schools could retain their independence in curriculum matters and staff appointments. If endowments were insufficient, the school had to become a 'controlled' school entirely responsible to the Local Education Authority. The proposal for a New Town at Stevenage, with the likely consequence that any grammar school would need to increase in size, complicated the issue.

After prolonged negotiations between the Governors, Trinity College and the County Council, a compromise was agreed upon. In 1948 it was resolved that Alleyne's would become a County 'controlled' Grammar School, remaining single-sex and on the same site. The County Council would fund any and all improvements required to comply with both the Education Act and the implications of the New Towns Act. Trinity's Endowment was cut by nearly two thirds, with the school being allowed to retain one third over and above the usual County funding, and the remaining money provisionally allocated to the establishment of a girls' grammar school in the town. The loss of the endowment required an Act of Parliament to amend the Charity Laws. The bulk of Thomas Alleyne's legacy was 'lost forever – confiscated' – as the Headmaster noted. The Girls' Grammar School eventually began life at the Grange.

I had taken the Scholarship Exam in 1945 and went to Alleyne's in the Autumn of that year. The Exam was held in the Assembly Hall and was followed by an Oral Examination in the room between the old

The Grammar School

Gymnasium/Class Room and the Masters' Common Room. This was conducted by Headmaster Thorne (just about to retire) and the man about to replace him as headmaster, W T Workman.

My schooling had started just next door at St Nicholas' Primary School in 1939, and continued, age seven, at the County Elementary School in Letchmore Road. Although the classrooms were ancient and the outdoor lavatories primitive at St Nicholas', kindly and diligent teachers eased us through the traumas of early schooldays. Sums and learning to write were still done with pencil on slate. The most up-to-date building in the school was across the playground under a mound – a large air-raid shelter. Cosy and relatively dry, I sat clutching my gas mask and a tin of 'emergency' rations. We happily decamped there during the occasional air-raid or rather the siren warning of an air-raid, because enemy aircraft never seemed to put in an appearance. My mother had thoughtfully packed my tin with coloured, icing-sugar covered biscuits which more than compensated for the disruptive effects of the air-raid.

Letchmore Road Boys School, whose buildings were still intact in 2005, provided sterner challenges in the shape of tough kids from the Stevenage Council estates. It also had a larger-than-life headmaster in the shape and sound of the roaring Mr Roach, a portly, rubicund-faced man who strode around with a purposeful air. He seems to have been an Officer in the Alleyne's Air Training Corps, which was also open to boys from the town. He can be seen in the photograph on p88 of *An Innings Well Played* in the centre of the Air Training Corps for 1942. Miss White, a teacher at Letchmore Road in 1945, recalls Mr Roach's 'sort of Victorian, chauvinistic attitude to women.' 'You women,' he said, 'I treat you like little flowers.' Miss White was excused playground duty, but went with Mr Clark to do dinner duty and just stood around while Mr Roach roared at the boys. His job seemed to be going round the classrooms doing mental arithmetic and getting a line of boys outside his room. 'To my room,' he would thunder. Her class of seven-year olds 'either went red with fear or white with fear. If they didn't get it right, or weren't quick enough, he tended to grind his teeth at them ... Goodness, they got good at mental arithmetic.' On one occasion one boy had riled him beyond teeth-grinding. This child was gripped by the chin between Mr Roach's finger and thumb and pushed from the front to the rear of the classroom. 'You, do you know what you are? You are the scum of the earth, boy!' With a survival instinct which did him credit, the boy noticed an open window at the back of the classroom. Evading the chin grip, he dived straight through the window into a flower bed and, regaining his feet, dashed off home. Later that day, the boy's formidable mother arrived at the school to remonstrate with Mr Roach.

156

If I were a Blackbird ...

By the time I came to take the Scholarship Exam from Letchmore Road School, I seemed to have run through their teaching material. I would have quite liked to work on one of the little garden plots which were north of the playground and cultivated by older boys who were staying on at school until they reached leaving age. Instead, I was set to remedial teaching to help the reading of one or two unlucky lads or allowed to work on my paintings under the supervision of Miss Ashworth.

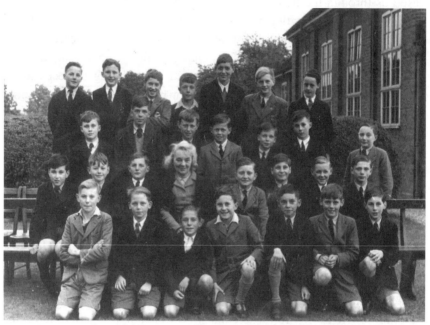

Fig 84 – The entry class of 1945 posed to the left of the school hall and grouped around our form teacher, Mrs Haggis.
Back row, left to right : Charlie Kitchener, Ralph (Doggy) Seal, Sam Glenn, Michael Tomlinson, (Gudger) Carter, Walter Coward, John Moore.
Row 2 : Brian Boorman, John Trussell, 'Nobby' Baker, Terry Plum, Ralph White, Reg. Horsnell, Gerald Barnes.
Row 3 : 'Bunny' Warren, John Austin, Ray Hopwood, Mrs Haggis, Phillip Day, P Smith, Ian Stephenson, John Whiteman.
Front row : Derek Woods, Tom Bridger, 'Tessa' Chamberlain, the Author, 'Bud' Welch, Michael Summers, Brian Creasey.

MASTERS AND MISTRESSES

At Alleyne's a new style of education awaited me. The shape of the day was in the hands of a few dedicated staff. Charles (W C) and Betty (Bet) Jones had joined the school in the 'thirties; Charles in 1935 and Bet in 1939. Nicknamed Pa and Ma Bung, they were the god-fathers of the school. Charles taught History mainly through elegant précis which he dictated to us. He was an excellent cricket and hockey coach as well as an ideal PT teacher, quietly encouraging, imparting confidence to timid boys and himself a highly talented batsman. Bet Jones, a County hockey player herself, was a lady of infinite warmth and kindness. I got to be rather fond of making meticulous coloured maps of the varieties of vegetation, levels of rainfall and mountain ranges, lowlands and rivers for Geography homework. Charles Jones later became headmaster after Francis Cammaerts took up the post of Principal at Leicester Teacher Training College. Old Boys who were pupils during Mr Jones' reign all look back on the era with great affection; it is a measure of the man that he was the only Headmaster to be habitually referred to by his nickname 'Pa Bung'.

Fig 85 – Charles Jones aka Pa Bung, headmaster 1961–68, with the school hockey team for 1953. The author is on the extreme right of the picture.

My conversion to a scientist I owe to Jack Starkey. His enthusiasm for chemistry and biology, his facility at offering clear explanations and his dexterity in making things work were his great strengths. Although I had some yearnings for the Arts and a fondness for English Literature, science looked the more certain avenue to the future and a career.

Jack Starkey was appointed to the staff in 1934, the year I was born; he came with a reputation as a swimmer and soon introduced life-saving into the school's swimming programme. This entailed a motor coach ride in one of Mr Chandler's North Star coaches to Letchworth public swimming baths. The water in these baths was, in all likelihood, obtained from melting glaciers, so arctic was their atmosphere. The acquatically-disadvantaged amongst us, of which I was certainly one, travelled with a dread anticipation of the treats ahead. Jack had a memorable way of

Fig 86 – Advert for North Star Coaches. The Garage was opposite the Astonia Cinema and in Letchmore, not Letchmere Road. (From 1946 Official Guide to Stevenage.)

starting swimming races, perhaps acquired in his Royal Navy days. To the contestants he would bark: 'I shall say are you ready, on your marks and then go.' The command then emerged in a rapid staccato on a rising crescendo, so that the last few words were emitted in a bellowed blur: 'Are you ready – on your marks – go!!' Jack took great pleasure in teaching carpentry, patiently coaching ham-fisted boys towards the goal of the perfect dove-tail joint.

In 1941 Jack Starkey was claimed by the Navy but rejoined the School Staff after the war. He served until his retirement in 1971, becoming Deputy Headmaster in 1961 and doyen of the School's Science Society. The Society had been founded in 1935 and held meetings in the Old Library on alternate Mondays during the Winter and Spring terms 'to discuss weighty topics not directly related to any examination syllabus.' The Old Library pre-war had an open fire and shields on the walls listing in white and gold the school's academic and sporting achievements. Frank Slow, the Senior Maths and Physics master presided at Society Meetings. In 1937 he talked to the Society about 'Radioactivity and its possibilities,' explaining that one pound of uranium could, in theory, power a liner across the Atlantic but that the slowness of atomic disintegrations would mean the journey would take about eight billion years. The year before Jack Starkey had spoken about 'The Theory of Evolution and chromosomes as carriers of inherited characteristics'. Jack died in Letchworth in 2005.

Fig 87 – Photo of Jack Starkey and George Partridge (on right) with 1952 swimming team (courtesy of Richard Stephens).

GEORGE PARTRIDGE

The most memorable of the other masters was George Partridge, who very nearly persuaded me through his eloquent exposition of the English Classics that I might base a career on a very small talent for literature. George, as described by De Salis and Stephens[26] was 'a medieval monarch and the Wizard of Oz to the younger boys and to the older, Renaissance Man and Superman.' He loomed so large because he was a ubiquitous presence: teaching English, Music, Art and Architecture, directing the School Orchestra, running scare-crow like around the hockey pitch wildly brandishing his stick, painting scenery for the school play, organising the annual swimming gala which ended with his own unique diving display, and arriving at school in a variety of vintage cars, topped by a monstrous, drop-head Sunbeam Talbot.

As a boy, George had attended Alleyne's in 1918. Rather small and weighing only four stone, he was immediately chosen to play the part of Tiny Tim in a production of *A Christmas Carol*. In *An Innings Well Played*[26], George recalls going to Morning Assembly in the old schoolroom which could just accommodate the 50 or so boys and four masters – the total complement of the school. It was often called the 'chapel' because it had been used in 1913 for Holy Communion during the renovation of St Nicholas' Church. During one chemistry class in which they were testing for the production by a chemical mixture of the gas hydrogen sulphide, George managed to render himself unconscious by sniffing too much of it, instead of bubbling it through a detection apparatus which would show a colour change. The next day the chemistry master arranged a reading 'especially for Partridge' from Oldham's Chemistry textbook:

Fig 88 – George Partridge and the school orchestra and choir around 1949. Between the windows can be seen the Memorial Board to the Fallen Alleynians of 1939–1945. George is standing on the left of the back row, two from the left is R Munnings, four from the left G J King, seventh from the left J S Arnold and to the right of the double-bass, Derek Woods.
In the middle row of instrumentalists on the far left is Phillip Day (violin). Fifth from the left is ? Brown (trombone), seventh from the left Michael Rayner (violin), eighth from the left and standing is the Author (violin) and on the far right is Ison (violin). The drummer is D Watson (courtesy Richard Stephens).

'When the tap is turned on, hydrogen sulphide gas is released, a sickly sweet odour of rotten eggs which is fatal to birds.'

Eventually George Partridge returned to the school as a member of staff after serving in the RAF. His musical abilities were by then well known, for he had been appointed organist and choirmaster of Aston Church in 1938. At the school he quickly built on the musical foundations laid by the previous music master, Thomas Hassard. A choir was re-established and a school orchestra started. By dint of being the longest serving violinist in this squad, I was eventually credited as its leader, although my feeble musical skills scarcely merited the title. George, the choir and the orchestra can be seen trapped by the camera in the Main Hall in the photograph from around 1949. George regularly put on a Holy Week Service which combined readings from a particular gospel, hymns, songs and classical interludes. George often sang the part of the Evangelist during a performance which soon became known as 'George's Passion.'

In 1945 George, still in the RAF, was travelling by rail through Stevenage. Learning from a fellow Old Boy on the train that the Headmaster, H P Thorne, was about to retire, he offered to paint a portrait for the school. The oil painting of Thorne was initially hung in the old library at the school. Thorne told him during the sittings that his successor as headmaster, W T Workman, was very worried about the staffing. There would be nobody to take English or Scripture, nobody to take Music since Mr Hassard was leaving, and nobody to take Art as Mr Jones would be required to concentrate on History, Games and PT. He then asked what George intended to do after he left the Air Force. George hoped to continue a teaching career specialising in English, Music and Art, with some Scripture. Both came to the obvious conclusion and this was the only interview George had for his post at Alleyne's. He was the first Old Alleynian to return to the school as a master.

For many years, George took the whole school in successive periods on Friday afternoons (Junior, Middle and Senior) and followed this with an orchestra rehearsal at 4 pm. 'And where were you last week, boy?' 'I'm afraid I was sick, Sir.' 'Did you say you were six, boy?' was one of his frequent sallies to keep our attention.

In Art and Architecture classes he would whistle up lightning sketches of Corinthian capitals or Doric columns, or for the human form, a vivid delineation of Bobby Charlton in the act of kicking the ball straight at you. Architecture was supplemented by tours in his car to see cathedrals, churches or other classic buildings. At Easter, 1950, there was a protracted cycling tour with Form V with us on our sports bikes and George on a decrepid pre-war machine.

If I were a Blackbird ...

Fig 89 – Dardy Williams (far right) and the rugby team and A S Biggerstaff. Alleyne's switched from soccer to rugby in 1954. Headmaster Francis Cammaerts invited Dardy to take charge of the change-over. (Courtesy of Richard Stephens).

DARDY WILLIAMS AND THE RICHES

Arithmetic, Algebra and Geometry were taught to us with great flair by another ex-RAF man, 'Dardy' Williams (JDW). He had come to the school after a distinguished war serving as a navigator on Lancaster bombers, expecting to teach Latin and Greek. He had trained at a Theological College. However, the Headmaster was teaching Latin, and Greek was not on the syllabus. He had perforce to turn his hand to other things such as Mathematics and Geography. Dardy was born in 1915 during the Dardanelles campaign in the First World War and the nickname stuck with him ever since. In 2002 he was still living in Stevenage with his wife.

French, especially oral French, was my bugbear subject. In 1945 it was taught by Mrs Rich, George Rich's wife – small, smart and efficient, a blonde tartar on high heels who scared us to death. Worryingly, she was teaching us only until her husband was released from war duties and could take over. He was rumoured to be working with the French Resistance, so if his wife was this tough, how much tougher would he be? Our fears were groundless. George Rich turned out to be a courteous, gentle man, quiet and conscientious. I would like to say that my spoken French improved immeasurably, but alas it was not so.

The Grammar School

NISI DOMINUS FRUSTRA

The three schools at Stevenage, Stone and Uttoxeter all use the same school motto: 'Nisi Dominus Frustra' – Unless the Lord build the house, they labour in vain that build it. Headmaster Hubert Thorne incorporated this motto into his school song, first written as an 'Ode to the School' in 1922 and subsequently set to music by Thomas Hassard.

1

'Fifteen hundred and fifty eight,
Ere Bess to the throne ascended!
"What shall I do," quoth his Reverence true,
"For my fame when life is ended?"
              Alleyne, Alleyne,
          Quoth the Reverend Thomas Alleyne.

2

"Stevenage, Stone and Uttoxeter too –
"Schools at them all will I found, sir!
"but Stevenage ever's the home that I love,
"I'll be buried in Stevenage ground, sir!
              "Stevenage, Stevenage,
I'll be buried in Stevenage ground, sir!"

3

Tudor, Stuart and Hanover men,
Carving an Empire's renown O –
Scions of Alleyne's have watched them pass
Rolling North from London town O –
              Mail coach, rail coach,
Rolling North from London town O.

4

Years roll onward, and youth has fled
And you're facing life's battle for fame, lad;
Think of the school by the King's highway
That taught you to play the game, lad?
              Alleyne's! Alleyne's!
That taught you to play the game, lad!

5

So come let us sing till the rafters ring
To the praise of all honest endeavour
For Honour and Truth and an Innings well played –
              "Dominus, Dominus,
"Nisi Dominus Frustra" for ever!

AFTERWORD

This book was written in part to provide my grandchildren with a picture of rural North Hertfordshire in the years towards the end, and soon after, the Second World War. This was the world in which I grew up. In many ways, this was a grim period for Britain. The hardships of the war were followed by a long spell of shortages and rationing, utility furniture and power cuts. One of my granddaughters, aged seven, asked to consider how grim war-time Britain may have been, replied confidently: 'Oh yes, Granny, I know. Everything was in black and white then.' As indeed the newsreels prove. It seemed appropriate to use illustrations in the book, whether photographs of relatives long dead, local footballing heroes playing for Stevenage Town FC, views of the old railway station or fire station or of dwellings and idiosyncratic corners of the town and countryside, in black and white. The pictures I have chosen have helped my recall of much of the detail in the book but also their dramatic *chiaroscuro* encouraged their rendering in pen and ink.

The chapters are a retrospective of a period which ended long before cynicism over politics, crass materialism and a superfluity of material wealth began to hold sway; a look back to a time when the overthrow of an obscene tyranny and the election of a Labour Government gave hope in Britain of renewal, greater social justice and a securer future – in Tony Benn's diaries: 'The years of hope'. This perspective has perhaps biased my history, coloured it with nostalgia, led to a partiality which has edited out some of the harsh realities of the times. Yet personal histories of a particular time in a particular place are bound to be partial. We each of us catch merely a glimpse of 'real' events as they quickly fade. Even if one could record them fresh, preserve them in amber, they would still be one person's subjective view distorted by his or her prejudices, coloured by his or her sensibility. With the passing of the years an internal censor will filter out certain details, will have smoothed out incongruities or added false memories to consolidate the picture.

So, if a time-machine were to carry you back to Stevenage just after the war is this how the place would have been? Would events have been like this? Can we revisit the past at all realistically or is 'The past a foreign country, where things are done differently', as L P Hartley maintained? A writer of a local history hopes he can create some feel for how it was, but the result will inevitably be an edited version, not the past as it was experienced. Even if we try to resist the rosy hindsight which fogs memory and adds a nostalgic gloss to events long gone, too much detail will have been lost and many painful emotions evaporated to leave a filtered, simplified and sanitised version of the past. Memories are not simply stored away unused and uncorrupted by time. The strongest memories are likely to have been replayed from time to time in conscious experience, each replay subtly altering the recorded message.

Daniel Schacter[28] emphasises how readily we forget and distort our past memories. As he points out: 'We do not record our experiences the way a camera records them. We extract key elements from our experiences and store them. We then reconstruct our experiences rather than retrieve copies of them. Sometimes, in the process of reconstructing we add feelings, beliefs or even knowledge we obtained after the experience. We bias our memories of the past by attributing to them emotions or knowledge we acquired after the event. 'Consistency biases' can lead us to rewrite past feelings and beliefs so they resemble what we feel and believe now. But I hope 'my Stevenage' will be recognisable to anyone who knew the old town, aided by the factual material available in old programmes, newspaper cuttings, my mother's diaries, Lummy's scrapbook, and the other sources which greatly helped me to write this book. The intentions were to entertain, injecting a little humour here and there. To provide some insight into the Stevenage of those days, realising that a full understanding would only be possible if the mindset of that era with its own preoccupations could be recovered. Or should I, echoing Alain-Fournier, confess that I do not know whether it is the town itself I miss or the times in the past I spent there.

David Wallis
August 2005

REFERENCES

1   Clare, John; *Collected Poems*; ed JW Tibble, JM Dent, London – 1

2   Spenser, Edmund; *Epithalamion* – 1

3   Thomas, Edward; *Tall Nettles*, Collected Poems; Faber & Faber; 1945 – 2

4   Hoskins, W G; *The making of the English Landscape*; Hodder & Stoughton; London; 1955 – 4, 19

5   Spicer, CM; *Tyme out of mind*; CM Spicer & DM de Salis; 1984 – 4

6   Hine, R; *Hitchin Worthies. Four Centuries of English Life*; George Allen & Unwin; 1932 – 4, 6

7   Trow-Smith, R; *The History of Stevenage*; The Stevenage Society; 1958 – 7, 12

8   Ashby, M; *The Book of Stevenage*; Barracuda Books; Buckingham; 1982 – 8, 10, 12, 113

9   Farris HON; *Symonds Green*; The Stevenage Society (Local History); 1982 – 8, 10

10 Orlans, H; *Stevenage: A Sociological study of a new town*; Hodder & Stoughton; London; 1952 – 8, 12, 35, 36, 42, 43, 44, 47, 50, 52

11 Methold, E V; *Notes on Stevenage and Baldock*; St Albans, Herts – 12

12 Appleton, M; *Stevenage in Old Photographs*; 1993 – 12, 21, 23, 54, 81

13 Clare, John; *The Skylark* – 14

14 Clare, John; *Bird Poems*; The Folio Society; London; 1980 – 14, 16, 18, 19

15 *Herts Express*; 4 May 1946 – 45

16 *The Times*; 14 May 1946 – 48

17 Subsequently Lord Chancellor in the post-war Labour administration – 58

18 www.family.history.dial.pipex.com/culpin1.html – 59

19 Dickens, Charles; *Christmas Stories*; Everyman's Library, JM Dent & Sons; London; 1933 – 64

20 *An Autobiography, Occupational Psychology*; 23, 140–152; 1949 – 68

References

21   *An Examination of Tropical Neurasthenia*; Culpin; Proc Roy Soc Med; 911;
       1933 – 71

22   *A Study of Telegraphists' Cramp*; Smith, Culpin & Farmer; Ind Health Res
       Board Rep No 43; 1927 – 72

23   *The Nervous Temperament in Industry*; Smith & Culpin; Ind Health Res Board
       Rep No 61; 1930 – 73

24   *The Occupational Neuroses (including Miner's Nystagmus)*; Proc Roy Soc
       Med; 655; 1933 – 73

25   *The changing face of Stevenage High Street, 1837–1997 – 106*

26   *An Innings well played. The story of Alleyne's School Stevenage*; (Stevenage)
       Old Boys' Association; De Salis, Dorothy & Stephens, Richard; 1989
       – 140, 154, 159

27   *Happy are thy men. The story of Alleyne's Grammar School Stevenage*;
       Alleyne's Old Boys' Association; 1958 – 140

28   Schacter, Daniel; *The seven sins of memory. How the mind forgets and
       remembers*; Souvenir Press, 2003. – 165

INDEX

169

Index

Index